# GATHERING STORM

Also by Morris Dees

A Season for Justice: The Life and Times of
Civil Rights Lawyer Morris Dees
(with Steve Fiffer)

Hate on Trial: The Case Against America's
Most Dangerous Neo-Nazi
(with Steve Fiffer)


Also by James Corcoran

Bitter Harvest: The Birth of Paramilitary
Terrorism in the Heartland

# GATHERING STORM

## America's Militia Threat

## Morris Dees

with James Corcoran

HarperCollins*Publishers*

HarperCollins books may be purchased for educational, business or sales promotional use. For information please write: Special Markets Department, HarperCollins Publishers, Inc., 10 East 53rd Street, New York, NY 10022.

FIRST EDITION

Designed by C. Linda Dingler

ISBN 0-06-017403-X

96 97 98 99 00 ❖/RRD 10 9 8 7 6 5 4 3 2 1

*For*
*Elizabeth Dees*
*my wife and friend*
*and*
*Richard Cohen*
*my law partner who has*
*fought these battles with me*

Four score and seven years ago our fathers brought forth on this continent a new nation, conceived in Liberty, and dedicated to the proposition that all men are created equal.

Now we are engaged in a great civil war, testing whether that nation, or any nation so conceived and so dedicated, can long endure.

Abraham Lincoln
*November 19, 1863*

# Contents

*Photographs follow page 176.*

# Author's Note

This is the story of a very dangerous movement, one the public knows almost nothing about. To some it might read like fiction, but, unfortunately, it is all true.

Much of what I write about, I learned from close contact with many of the far-right extremists who are behind the militia movement. Some of the information was gained through undercover operations I cannot reveal. Many of those involved will be surprised to find their words and actions publicly exposed.

When Timothy McVeigh and Terry Nichols were indicted for the Oklahoma City bombing, the *New York Times* said in an editorial that the "case may turn out to be much simpler than many had thought. . . . [T]wo former buddies nursing hatred of the government carried out the most destructive act of domestic terrorism in the nation's history. That is reassuring in the sense that there may be no organized conspiracy to carry out other terrorist bombings."

It's not that simple. The chain of events that led to the Oklahoma City bombing dates back to the early 1980s. It is a continuing threat that promises to cause further destruction.

Morris Dees
*Rolling Hills Ranch*
*Mathews, Alabama*
*January 2, 1996*

# About the Authors

**MORRIS DEES** is chief trial counsel for the Southern Poverty Law Center and its Militia Task Force. He is the author of *A Season for Justice* and *Hate on Trial* with Steve Fiffer. His cases were the subjects of an NBC Movie of the Week and a Bill Moyers PBS special. He lives with his wife in Mathews, Alabama.

**JAMES CORCORAN** is an associate professor and chairman of the communications department at Simmons College in Boston. He is the author of *Bitter Harvest,* which won both the Golden Pen Award and the Gustavus Myers Center Award for Outstanding Book on the subject of human rights. His reporting on the Gordon Kahl case, which was the basis for *Bitter Harvest,* was nominated for a Pulitzer Prize. *Bitter Harvest* was also an NBC made-for-television movie. He lives in Somerville, Massachusetts.

# GATHERING STORM

# Introduction

Louis Beam minced no words.

"I warn you calmly, coldly, and without reservation that over the next ten years you will come to hate government more than anything in your life," Beam, a spokesman for the Aryan Nations, told his audience of 160 white men. They ranged from white supremacists to pro-gun extremists, meeting at an invitation-only gathering two months after FBI sharpshooters killed Randy Weaver's wife and son on Ruby Ridge in Idaho. They called themselves patriots.

"The federal government in north Idaho has demonstrated brutally, horribly, and with great terror how it will enforce its claim that we are religious fanatics and enemies of the state," added Beam, his voice rising with each word. "We must, in one voice, cry out that we will not tolerate their stinking, murdering, lying, corrupt government.

"Men, in the name of our Father, we are called upon to make a decision, a decision that you will make in the quietness of your heart, in the still places of the night," Beam continued. "As you lie on your bed and you look up at the ceiling tonight, you must answer the question: Will it be liberty or will it be death?

"As for me," he concluded in the words of Patrick

Henry to thunderous applause, "give me liberty or give me death."

At this gathering, now known as the Rocky Mountain Rendezvous, held on October 23–25, 1992, at a YMCA in Estes Park, Colorado, plans were laid for a citizens' militia movement like none this country has known. It is a movement that already has led to the most destructive act of domestic terrorism in our nation's history. Unless checked, it could lead to widespread devastation or ruin.

"We bear the torch of light, of justice, of liberty, and we will be heard," Beam shouted over the cheers of his audience. "We will not yield this country to the forces of darkness, oppression, and tyranny."

His face pockmarked, his hair slicked down, and speaking in a manner that evoked images of Adolf Hitler, Beam continued, "So if you believe in the truth, if you believe in justice, then join with us. We are marching to the beat of the same drum. The beat of that drum, like those heard at Valley Forge and at Gettysburg, has called good men everywhere to action."

I first met Louis Beam in a Texas federal court in 1981 when I forced him to stop harassing Vietnamese fishermen in Galveston Bay and to disband his 2,500-member paramilitary army. He later made the FBI's Ten Most Wanted list after being indicted, along with twelve other avowed racists, for seditious conspiracy against the United States. After his acquittal by an all-white Arkansas jury, Beam marched from the Fort Smith courthouse and saluted the Confederate memorial in the town square. "To hell with the federal government," he shouted to his supporters.

When I took Beam to court, his appeals to white

supremacy and violence were the central tenets of his message. "Enough of this backing up and retreating," Louis Beam told the members of his Texas Emergency Reserve militia in 1981. "Enough of this lip service and no action. It's time to begin to train. It is time to begin to reclaim this country for white people. Now I want you to understand that they're not going to give it back to us. If you want it, you're gonna have to get it the way the founding fathers got it—Blood! Blood! Blood! The founding fathers shed their blood to give you this country, and if you want to hold on to it, you're gonna have to shed some of yours.

"Never let any race but the white race rule this country."

That racist message limited his popular appeal. Similar messages from others met with similarly limited success. Few people rallied to the likes of the Posse Comitatus, The Order, or the Aryan Nations when, during the farm crisis of the 1980s, they tried to bring embittered farmers into the fold by telling them that a Communist–Jewish–federal government conspiracy was responsible for destroying the family farm and that the only way they could protect their homes, families, and way of life was to join with the radical right in a battle for survival.

Few people rallied to the white supremacists when they echoed a similar theme to gain converts among blue-collar workers in the Northeast suffering from the decline of the steel industry. And few people rallied to them when they repeated variations on that theme during conflicts between whites and Native Americans over fishing rights in Wisconsin and between environmentalists and loggers over the spotted owl in the Northwest.

Their antigovernment theme resonated with some

individuals during the 1980s, but their strident racist and anti-Semitic rhetoric kept Beam and the others at the fringes of the debate.

Nonetheless, the leader of the neo-Nazi National Alliance, William Pierce, who was never an optimist about the prospects for a white revolution, made a jarring prediction: "The wind is shifting. The 1990s are going to be different."

Today is different. Beam and his militia followers are repackaging their message. They downplay racism and focus on people's fear and anger. The fear of, and anger at, a government that overregulates, overtaxes, and, at times, murders its citizens. The fear of, and anger at, a government that is insensitive, uncaring, and callous to the needs of its people. The fear of, and anger at, a government that takes away a person's right to bear arms so that the country is vulnerable to domination by a New World Order.

Tens of thousands of people are hearing the message and thousands are joining their movement, many unaware that Beam and his fellow travelers are helping to set the agenda.

They are just the type of people racists and neo-Nazi leaders have long been after. They are mainly white and middle class. Most hold jobs, own homes, wear their hair short, don't use drugs, and, for one reason or another, they hate our government.

It is that virulent hatred of the federal government that is driving the militia movement, while at the same time masking its insidious racist underpinnings.

The racist message is never far from the surface. Timothy McVeigh condemned the federal government to anyone who would listen prior to the bombing of the Alfred P. Murrah Federal Building in Oklahoma City. His bible was *The Turner Diaries*, a fictional story of an

Aryan revolt that begins with the bombing of a federal building and ends with the mass annihilation of Jews and blacks.

Hatred for the federal government is not just being preached by professional racists. Americans get a daily dose of antigovernment venom from radio talk shows, respectable lobbying organizations, and even members of Congress that competes in viciousness, mean-spiritedness, and hatefulness with anything said or written by members of the extremist movement. It has helped to create a climate and culture of hate, a climate and culture in which invective and irresponsible rhetoric is routinely used to demonize an opponent, legitimize insensitive stereotypes, and promote prejudice.

This point is not missed by the ideological thinkers behind this frightening movement. William Pierce, the author of *The Turner Diaries*, pointed out to his followers in 1994 that "most people aren't joiners, but millions of white Americans who five years ago felt so cowed by the government and [the Jewish-] controlled media that they were afraid to agree with us are becoming fed up, and their exasperation is giving them courage."

Hatred and distrust of government are running so deep that many militia members believe that federal agents exploded the Oklahoma City bomb and murdered innocent children to discredit the militia movement and to facilitate passage of an antiterrorist crime bill. They want to reclaim their America with bullets and blood, not ballots and bluster. Ammunition stockpiles are brimming full as militia groups across the country prepare for a war "to protect citizens from their government." John Trochmann, founder of the Militia of Montana, said, "We don't want bloodshed. We want to use the ballot box and the jury box. We don't want to go to the cartridge box. But we will if we have to."

I have had an all-too-close relationship with the type of fanatics who are seeking to exploit the militia movement. Because of my work against them, they have tried to kill me. In 1983, they burned the office where I work. In 1984, they came on my property to shoot me. In 1986, they plotted to blow me up with a military rocket. In 1995, they tried to build a bomb like the one that destroyed the Oklahoma City federal building to level my office. Twelve have been imprisoned for these crimes. Four await trial.

Since 1979, my associates and I at the Klanwatch Project of the Southern Poverty Law Center have been monitoring organized racists and far-right extremists through an intensive intelligence operation. Our investigative staff gathers its information from public sources, recorded speeches and publications of the leaders and groups we monitor, law enforcement sources, court depositions, Internet postings, informers, and, in some cases, carefully conducted undercover operations. Our data, computerized and cross-referenced, now contain 12,094 photographs and videos and 65,891 entries on individuals and events. We share much of this information with more than six thousand law enforcement sources through our quarterly *Intelligence Report*. Prosecutors have used information our intelligence staff has gathered to help convict more than twenty white supremacists.

In October 1994, I wrote Attorney General Janet Reno to alert her to the danger posed by the growing number of radical militia groups. I had learned that some of the country's most notorious racists and neo-Nazis were infiltrating the leadership of the so-called citizen militias.

They are men who believe that we are in the middle of a "titanic struggle" between white Aryans, God's chosen people, and Jews, the children of Satan.

Their blueprint for winning the struggle is found in *The Turner Diaries*, the story of a race war that leads to the downfall of our government.

I told the attorney general that this "mixture of armed groups and those who hate is a recipe for disaster."

Six months later, 169 people lay dead. Whether the federal government, with its vast resources, could have done something to prevent the bombing if they had taken my warning seriously is something I can't claim to know.

But I do know the Oklahoma City tragedy was not an isolated event. Similar fanatics with close ties and fueled by the same missionary zeal are at work.

In June 1995, an open letter to me was published in *Resistance*, a widely circulated newsletter of an extremist group. It began:

> *Dear Morris:*
>
> Our future is Oklahoma City. I have a deep and abiding faith in the ultimate depravity of mankind. There will be no brotherhood, Morris, only racial hatred and contempt and fear and loathing and rage until one side or the other in this titanic struggle has perished completely. Count on it, my friend. There is a cruel, cold time coming.
>
> We can make your liberal New World Order pay for every inch of America in violence and pain and anguish until the ground is sodden with the blood and the tears of my dying race; until the land and the skies of North America are so poisoned with the emissions of the White man's death struggle that you and your kind cannot breathe.

America is at a very serious crossroads. We are deeply divided along racial, political, economic, and class lines. Fear, anger, and paranoia prevail all too often.

The militia warriors fear the most and hate the most. They have killed before. And they will kill again.

# Death on Ruby Ridge
1

It was something that didn't happen that sparked the militia movement and set into motion the chain of events that is still unfolding.

In February 1991, Randy Weaver didn't appear for his trial on felony charges of selling two sawed-off shotguns to an informant for the Bureau of Alcohol, Tobacco, and Firearms. Instead, he, together with his wife Vicki, their son Samuel, two daughters Sara and Rachel, and family friend Kevin Harris, retreated to his cabin atop Ruby Ridge near Naples, Idaho.

An army veteran and a hardened survivalist, Weaver had stockpiled food, weapons, and ammunition for the inevitable day when "ZOG" would come for him. ZOG stands for Zionist Occupied Government, a term for the U.S. government used by racists and neo-Nazis to reflect the belief that the country is controlled by Jews. On that remote scrap of mountainside, Weaver and his family would defy the lackeys of ZOG and the New World Order and would wait for Yahweh's will to be done.

"Whether we live or whether we die," he told the U.S. attorney through his lawyer, "we will not obey your lawless government."

Later, as the standoff with the government wore on, Weaver told an interviewer, "[T]he only thing [the government] can take away from us is our life. Even if we die, we win. We'll die believing in Yahweh."

If it was Yahweh's will that they be taken home to sit at his side, so be it. It was Yahweh, after all, who brought the Weavers from the rolling corn fields surrounding their home in Cedar Falls, Iowa, to the pristine, pine-scented mountains of the Idaho panhandle. (The Weavers never referred to God because it was dog spelled backward. God was Yahweh; Jesus Christ was Yahshua.)

Soon after their marriage in 1971, the couple set out on a spiritual journey that would take them from the mainstream Baptist Church of their Iowa upbringing to the extreme edges of Christianity where they would discover, and embrace, the Israel Message of Christian Identity.

That message professes that white people are the true Israelites and that Jews and people of color are, respectively, "children of Satan" and "the beasts of the field." It maintains that America is the New Jerusalem and that the Constitution was derived from the Bible and given to the white Christian Founding Fathers by God. It contends the U.S. government is nothing more than an expansion of the Christian faith and that the first Ten Amendments of the Constitution (the Bill of Rights) and the Articles of Confederation are the only documents—aside from the Bible—that need be obeyed. The Israel Message also holds that only white Christian men are true sovereign citizens of the United States. All other Americans, it argues, are merely

Fourteenth Amendment "state" citizens, the creation of an illegitimate government.

Through Christian Identity, the Weavers learned the income tax was unconstitutional and desegregation of public schools was an effort to encourage interracial marriage. They learned that the federal government was controlled by a Jewish-led conspiracy of bankers who used the Internal Revenue Service and the Federal Reserve Board to manipulate the economy for personal gain. The same group, they were told, was tightening its grip on the news media, the courts, and the economy to hasten a one-world government that would one day enslave all white Christians.

Through Identity, the Weavers also came to accept the Bible as the literal word of Yahweh. And they came to understand what He was saying to them through the Scriptures.

They understood when, in Luke 22, Jesus said: "Let him who has no sword sell his robe and buy one."

They bought weapons. Lots of them. Two Ruger Mini-14 semiautomatics, a .223 rifle, a pump-action shotgun, a .38-caliber snub-nosed revolver, and a 9mm pistol. And a lot of ammunition.

The Weavers lived in a world where the "End-Times," as predicted in the book of Revelation, was approaching. Wars, rumors of wars, famines, pestilence, and diseases were sweeping the world and parts of America in their view. The evidence of that was in the newspapers they read and the television programs they watched. Soon there would be great discord throughout the land, people would riot in the streets, and ZOG would turn on all good Christians. It was time to seek out the holy place and join with other like-minded—and well-armed—Christians so they would have strength in numbers when Armageddon, the last great battle, came.

They understood the Biblical injunction in Matthew 24: "When ye therefore shall see the abomination of desolation, spoken of by Daniel the prophet, stand in the holy place: Then let them which be in Judea flee into the mountains."

In 1983, the Weavers migrated to the remote reaches of northern Idaho. There they built their cabin, high in the Selkirk Mountains. Constructed from plywood and two-by-fours, the cabin consisted of one large room and a sleeping loft; a generator supplied electricity, but there was no running water or indoor plumbing.

There they set down roots in a community that saw them as somewhat intense in their religious and political views, but welcomed them as hardworking, decent, and friendly folks. Good neighbors. Randy even ran for sheriff, promising to enforce only those laws the eight thousand or so residents of Boundary County wanted enforced. He received 102 of the some 400 votes cast in the two-person race.

The Weavers home-schooled their children, something they couldn't do in Iowa without a lot of hassles from government bureaucrats who wanted subjects taught that violated Yahweh's laws. Subjects such as sex education and race-mixing.

And, amid all the grandeur and beauty that is the Idaho panhandle, they found kindred spirits. They found the Aryan Nations.

The Aryan Nations compound, which was located sixty miles south of the Weavers' home, had been established in the mid-1970s by Richard Butler. A former aerospace engineer, Butler moved from California to Hayden Lake to escape the Jews, blacks, Hispanics, and other "alien scum" that he believed were contaminating the country and threatening to overwhelm the white majority. Like the Weavers, Butler held a man's race was his nation; neither should be polluted by contact with inferior individuals. He called for the establishment of an all-white nation in America's northwest. He believed a race war was both imminent and necessary to take back control of the U.S. government from the Jews and their black, brown, and yellow pawns. He encouraged his supporters to take up arms and prepare themselves for the coming of the Second American Revolution. And, like the Weavers, Butler justified his views through the hateful gospel of Christian Identity.

Although the Weavers never joined the Aryan Nations, they attended a number of the group's annual congresses and family day events. They enjoyed the kinship of fellow Identity Christians and the company of the people they met there. It was there that they met John and Carolyn Trochmann, who became close friends. It also was there that Randy met Gus Magisono, who said he needed sawed-off shotguns. The weapons would be used, he told Weaver, to forward the cause of Identity.

In October 1989, Weaver delivered two shotguns and was paid $300 by Magisono, who, in reality, was Kenneth Fadeley, a government informant. When the lawmen came for Randy, they offered him a deal: infiltrate the white supremacist movement as an FBI operative and the charges against him would be dropped. Weaver refused. He was indicted on gunrunning charges in December 1990.

When Weaver failed to appear for trial, a warrant for his arrest was issued. But the government wasn't anxious to confront Weaver. A month passed. Then six months. Then a year. Elisheba, the Weavers' third daughter, was born.

"He's not the only one living up there," Ron Evans, the chief deputy marshal for Idaho, told a reporter more than a year into the standoff. "We have four children and a wife up there who have not been charged with any crimes."

What Evans didn't tell the reporter was that nine years earlier, as the newly assigned chief deputy marshal for North Dakota, he was witness to a similar episode that ended in disaster.

On February 13, 1983, on a lonely prairie road outside of Medina, North Dakota, Evans's superior, U.S. Marshal Kenneth Muir, three of his fellow deputies, and two local lawmen attempted to arrest Gordon Kahl. Kahl was a follower of Christian Identity and a member of the Posse Comitatus, a shadowy racist, anti-Semitic, antitax group that believes there is no legitimate form of government beyond the county level. He was convinced a Jewish-led conspiracy had infiltrated the federal government, the judicial system, and law enforcement, and was bent on destroying his white, Christian America. Much like Randy Weaver, Kahl was a True Believer. He believed he was engaged in a Holy War. And he repeatedly vowed he would kill anyone who tried to arrest him for failure to pay some $30,000 in taxes.

He kept that vow.

Nobody knows who fired the first shot. But after a fierce, thirty-second gun battle, Muir and one of his deputies, Robert Cheshire, lay dead. Four other men—three lawmen and Kahl's twenty-year-old son, who was not wanted by authorities—were critically wounded. Kahl was a fugitive.

For nearly five months, Kahl eluded one of the largest manhunts ever mounted by American law enforcement. During that time, he became a hero to many people. Ballads were written that sang the praises of Kahl and his stand against the government. No one seemed interested in the $25,000 reward that the government offered. Finally, during the first week of June, Kahl was traced to a farmstead in rural Arkansas where he was holed up in a bunkerlike house containing a small arsenal of weapons and ammunition. More than one hundred federal, state, and local law enforcement officers assaulted the building. When the firefight ended, a county sheriff and Kahl were dead.

A month later, white supremacists from across the country gathered at the Aryan Nations' congress where they hailed Kahl as the "first martyr of the Second American Revolution."

After the Kahl incident, U.S. marshals and FBI agents sat down to review the handling of the case. What they concluded was that people like Kahl and his associates would not respond to the logic of superior firepower. Unlike more conventional criminals such as drug lords or Mafia hit men, the Kahls of the world didn't care if they were outnumbered or outgunned. In some cases, they even wanted to die, to offer themselves as martyrs to their cause. The government found that Kahl and others like him, much like the individuals who would flock to the militia movement, are people who are estranged from the political process that we take for granted. They are people who see their government as the enemy and who believe its laws and legal system are used not to help and protect them, but to take away their rights, infringe on their beliefs, and destroy their way of life. They are people who respond to what they believe is a higher call. Rather than obey the laws, they resist them as a matter of principle. Even to the death.

As a result of the review, the U.S. Marshals Service established procedures that emphasized surveillance, containment, and negotiation over brute, Rambo-like, face-to-face confrontation.

"We spend hours on the pistol range qualifying with a weapon but the most important weapon is not on the hip, but in the head," said then U.S. Marshals Service Director Stanley Morris.

The new procedures worked. In 1984, approximately twenty-five marshals and local lawmen surrounded the Montana ranch of David Pederson, another Posse Comitatus member wanted for tax evasion. Pederson had barricaded himself in the house with several semiautomatic weapons. After a couple of hours of negotiation, marshals were able to take him into custody without firing a shot.

Then, in 1985, more than one hundred officers surrounded the compound of the Covenant, Sword and Arm of the Lord, a paramilitary wing of the Christian Identity religious group in Arkansas. The lawmen were there to arrest the group's leader, James Ellison, on weapons violations and charges of conspiring to overthrow the government.

After two tense days of negotiations, Ellison and his supporters, including scores of women and children, surrendered to authorities. More than one of the officers at the scene privately expressed relief over the strategy chosen by their superiors when, after entering the compound, they found automatic assault rifles, thousands of rounds of ammunition, grenades, antitank rockets and launcher, and a thirty-gallon drum of cyanide.

Why not follow the same strategy in the Weaver case?

The Marshals Service didn't need another botched arrest attempt that put innocent people in harm's way. Nor did it need to provide the white supremacist movement with any more martyrs.

They could wait, said Idaho Deputy Marshal Evans.

And they did.

For seventeen months the Marshals Service kept a watchful eye on the Weavers, whose friends—among them the Trochmanns—provided them with food and other essentials during the siege. Then, in August 1992, the marshals' plan unraveled.

On the twenty-first of that month, the marshals went up Ruby Ridge to conduct surveillance of the Weaver residence. They wore camouflage, not clothing or any insignia that identified them as law enforcement officials. As they were conducting their operations, they were detected by the Weavers' dog, Striker, who started to bark. Weaver, his fourteen-year-old son Sam, and family friend Kevin Harris heard the dog and set out from the cabin to investigate why he was causing such a fuss. Like the marshals, the Weavers and Harris were armed.

What happened next may never be known, but the weight of the evidence points to the following sequence of events. As Harris and Sam Weaver came toward the marshals, one of the marshals shot Striker so the dog would not give away their position. Outraged at seeing his dog gunned down, Sam fired toward the marshals. The exchange escalated, and U.S. Deputy Marshal William Degan and Sam Weaver were killed.

The next day, an FBI sharpshooter—operating under revised rules of engagement that allowed him to shoot any armed adult male leaving the cabin—fired a shot that blew away half the face of Weaver's forty-three-year-old wife Vicki as she stood in the doorway with a ten-month-old daughter in her arms. He said he had been aiming at Harris, but hit Vicki as she held open the door for her husband and Harris, who had gone to check on Sam's body in a shed near the cabin. Both Harris and Weaver were wounded by the sniper, Lon Horiuchi.

The next day, Sunday, the twenty-third of August, the government attempted to open negotiations with Weaver. He refused to speak to them.

He had been ambushed by the agents of the New World Order. They had murdered his son and his wife. In all likelihood they would murder his friend, his daughters, and him. They were his enemies. They were the enemies of Yahweh and Christian Identity.

For nearly fifty years the perverted beliefs of Christian Identity have percolated through the ranks of the racist movement. Identity is the theological thread that binds the diverse—and oftentimes feuding—segments of the racist movement into a whole cloth. It allows white-robed Klansmen to mingle with plaid-shirted Posse members, and camouflaged survivalists to rub shoulders with brown-shirted neo-Nazis.

But Identity isn't just about race or white supremacy. Like the theology of many fundamentalist and cult religious groups, Christian Identity's worldview extends into the secular world of politics and provides a tent big enough to incorporate the views of various extremist groups. It invites individuals who are extremely antigovernment, anti–law enforcement, antitax, antiabortion, antigay, antifeminist, anti–medical profession, antivaccination, pro-guns, pro–home schooling, pro–states' rights, and believers in an international one-world conspiracy that is about to take over America and the world. It welcomes persons who believe they have no place in a world that has become too secular, too immoral, and too modern.

Identity unifies them through a theology of hate. It brings them together, shoulder-to-shoulder, through its warped interpretations of the Bible that provide simple answers to complex questions and justify both the hate and the violence that too often follows from such views.

"There are some buzzwords and terms used by the anti-Christ forces . . . to describe a socially unaccept-able people," complained Identity Pastor Pete Peters, who, for more than twenty-two years, has been a prominent figure in the far-right movement. "The words and terms are: survivalist, racist, tax protester, militant, and right-wing extremist.

"But the gospel truth of the matter is these are the very type of people God has honored in the Bible," added Peters. "In fact, the Bible is about such people, heralding them as heroes and even role models for our children."

Those heroes and role models include Phinehas, who would be labeled a bigot and a racist by modern stan-dards. Peters wrote in his *Handbook for Survivalists, Racists, Tax Protesters, Militants, and Right-Wing Extre-mists:*

> Perhaps there was an organization in Phinehas' day known as the NAACP (National Association for the Advancement of Canaanite People). Perhaps there were pulpits proclaiming a more tolerant and socially accepted view, and government agencies crusading for "affirmative action." We really do not know. But we do know from the Bible . . . that the Israel people began to disobey God's law, accept integration, cul-tural exchange, and a type of interracial marriage, and thus were struck by a plague.

Phinehas was the one man who fought against racial treason in biblical times, said Peters, even to the point of killing an Israelite man and a Midianite woman who defied God's command and married. God honored Phinehas's stand against integration by stopping the plague. "Racism is a sin in the humanist religion, not in the true Christian faith based on the Bible," said Peters, whose taped Scriptures for America sermons can be heard on shortwave radio and found on the Internet. "There was a time in America when interracial marriage was against the law and integration was not only socially but religiously unacceptable. In those days, America had no racial problems nor a killing plague such as AIDS."

Peters also pointed to Gideon, the biblical figure who threshed his wheat by the winepress to keep it out of sight and out of the hands of tax collectors for the Midian conquerors. "Gideon was a tax protester who would today be condemned," said Peters. "Yet he is placed in both the Old and New Testaments of the Bible as a hero."

Gideon's story has a strong parallel to the United States, a country "invaded by hordes of illegal aliens and sons of the East who bleed a welfare system whose blood bank is the hearts of millions of laboring, over-taxed Americans," said Peters.

Then there are Shadrach, Meshach, and Abednego, who defied King Nebuchadnezzar's decree that all his subjects must bow before his golden image. "All obeyed the new additional government regulation except these three extremists," said Peters. "It was these three God honored."

But today's distorted humanistic religion known as Judeo-Christianity, said Peters, preaches that Americans not only must bow, they must also "file, report, register, pay, submit, remit, buckle up, get a sticker, take a test, get a license. Those Christian people who attempt to regain the inalienable God-given right protected by the Constitution are made to feel un-spiritual and un-Christian.

"Yet God has not changed and it was He who gave,

for our learning, the story of the three radicals standing in the name of their God when all others bowed."

And then there is the militant Jesus Christ, said Peters, who urged his apostles to arm themselves with swords, even if they had to sell their garments to do so. The sword in Jesus' day was equivalent to an M16 in our day, he said, and it is the duty of all Christians "not only to own one, but be able to use one."

It is through these and other interpretations of the Bible that Identity gives its followers a sense of divine guidance and approval to engage in racial hatred, bigotry, and murder. When Identity counsels "lawful" ways and means, it does not mean local, state, and federal statutes. It means God's Law. Literally. Therefore, if one accepts the Identity teaching that Jews are the children of Satan and people of color are subhuman, one can kill with a clear conscience. It is neither a sin nor is it against the law to murder a race-mixer when a person is simply following God's commands. Instead, it is virtuous. It is righteous.

"No, folks, it is not a perverse joy I take in the impending doom of the enemy," said James W. Bruggeman, an Identity pastor with the Stone Kingdom Ministries in Asheville, North Carolina. "It is a righteous joy!

"Wouldn't you rejoice if you saw vengeance being meted out to the perpetrators of the murderers of the Weavers out in Idaho?" he asked. "The righteous will rejoice when he sees the vengeance. [The righteous] shall wash his feet in the blood of the wicked."

At the time the militia movement was born, Christian Identity was seeking to form coalitions with fundamentalist Christians. Its leaders saw opposition to abortion and gay rights as well as advocacy of home schooling and Bible-based laws as common ground for both groups.

"While we do not agree with some of the doctrines espoused by other Christian action groups . . . it is time to temporarily lay aside certain differences and work for the common goal of taking America back for Christ," Pastor Bruggeman wrote in his ministry's newsletter, *The Christian Patriot Crusader,* in 1994. "Do not misunderstand. This is not to say that our doctrinal disagreements are not important. But let's be realistic. Let's focus on regaining America from the anti-Christs so that we can have the leisure time to debate doctrine with our Christian brethren."

But not all their Christian brethren.

Except for the fundamentalists, said Peters, "Today's modern, state approved, tax exempt Christianity is . . . a refined, palatable, goody, goody religion that fits well within the plans of the one world Communist conspirators, [and] is tenderly embraced by an effeminate world, and is socially accepted by a Christless, Lawless, Humanistic society."

There is nothing "goody, goody" or "tender" about Identity. It is a religion, a form of Christianity, that few churchgoers would recognize as that of Jesus, son of a loving God. It is a religion on steroids. It is a religion whose God commands the death of race traitors, homosexuals, and other so-called children of Satan. It is a postmillennium religion that believes Jesus Christ will return once God's law is established on earth following the Battle of Armageddon.

Identity adherents are preparing for that battle.

They advocate keeping a well-stocked arsenal and survival gear at the ready. Some have taken their weapons and survival gear and retreated into armed compounds or "covenant communities" such as Elohim City in Oklahoma and Ephraim's Forum in Arizona. There they await the coming Battle of Armageddon.

Once the battle begins, they will answer God's call to serve as Soldier-Saints, cleanse the world of all remaining anti-Christ forces, and then "rule and reign" with him once he establishes his pure, white Christian Kingdom on earth.

Many Identity leaders have been in the forefront of the extremist paramilitary movement since the 1960s. William Potter Gale, a former aide to General Douglas MacArthur and leading guerrilla strategist during World War II, and Robert DePugh, the millionaire founder of the ultra-rightist Minutemen, were early proponents of "unorganized militias" and fervent Identity believers. During the 1980s and into the 1990s, their efforts have been carried on by people like Louis Beam; Glenn and Stephen Miller, organizers of the White Patriot Party; Jim Ellison, founder of the Covenant, Sword and Arm of the Lord; and former Posse Comitatus leader James Wickstrom.

Identity's followers are people who practice what they preach.

The most violent episodes out of the racist right during the past fifteen years have erupted from Identity groups. Those episodes have left more than two dozen people dead.

U.S. Marshal Kenneth Muir, Deputy Marshal Bob Cheshire, and Lawrence County (Arkansas) sheriff Gene Matthews were killed in 1983 by Gordon Kahl, who saw the lawmen as Shabbas goys—agents doing the dirty work of his Jewish enemies.

In June 1984, Alan Berg, a Jewish radio talk show host in Denver, Colorado, was gunned down by members of The Order, a neo-Nazi group.

That same month, Lewis Bryant, a black Arkansas state trooper, was shot eleven times when he stopped a vehicle driven by Richard Wayne Snell, a member of

the Identity-steeped Covenant, Sword and Arm of the
Lord, for a minor traffic violation.

On April 15, 1985, Missouri highway patrolman Jim
Linegar was killed and another trooper severely
wounded after they stopped a van that belonged to
David Tate, a member of The Order who was on his way
to the Covenant, Sword and Arm of the Lord compound
located along the Missouri-Arkansas border. Tate was
captured after a six-day manhunt and is now serving a
life sentence.

In August 1992 at Ruby Ridge, it seemed to the government, one more lawman had fallen victim to yet
another Identity adherent, Randy Weaver.


By Wednesday, August 26, Weaver still had not responded
to the government's request for a dialogue. It was then
that James "Bo" Gritz approached the FBI and asked to
speak to Weaver. Gritz, a charismatic former Special
Forces commander in Vietnam, wanted to talk to Weaver
"soldier to soldier." It was the only way to end the standoff without more bloodshed, he said.

Gene Glenn, the FBI agent in charge, was leery.
Gritz was a loose cannon. One minute he was giving
press conferences promoting his candidacy for president on the ticket of the anti-Semitic Populist Party. In
1988, Gritz was briefly the party's vice presidential
candidate on a ticket that was headed by avowed
racist David Duke as the choice for president. And
when he wasn't giving press conferences, Gritz was
handing out "arrest warrants" that charged everyone
from Glenn to FBI Director William Sessions to Idaho
governor Cecil Andrus with the deaths of Degan and
Samuel Weaver.

Still, things were getting ugly. The crowd near the

roadblock had grown to nearly one hundred persons. It was a combustible blend of Aryan Nations followers, Identity adherents, skinheads, and local residents who believed the government was terribly wrong in its actions. And it was growing in anger as well as size. Individuals carried signs that read: WE'RE FED UP WITH THE FEDS, ZIONIST MURDERERS, and FBI BURN IN HELL. Others threatened to get even with the officers and chanted "Baby killer, baby killer," as lawmen passed by. Five skinheads were stopped near the government's encampment and arrested for carrying rifles and bayonets.

Glenn's decision on whether to bring in Gritz was made for him when, after hearing of Gritz's presence, Weaver asked to speak to him.

On August 28, Gritz, along with Vicki's friend Jackie Brown, went up the mountain. Gritz brought with him a letter from Identity Pastor Pete Peters. When Gritz and fellow movement activist Jack McLamb, a former police officer in Phoenix, Arizona, were en route to Ruby Ridge to try to intercede as negotiators on behalf of Weaver, Gritz had contacted Peters at his Scriptures for America Family Bible Camp in Colorado. Gritz told Peters that he felt a letter from an Identity minister of his stature could help convince Randy Weaver to talk to him.

At the time during the siege that he wrote the letter, Peters only knew of Samuel's death. The letter read:

> *Dear Randy:*
> Please know that the murder of your son has not gone unnoticed. Five hundred Christian Israelites from 40 states . . . are right now praying for you and the Gideon situation you face.
> Col. Bo Gritz and Jack McLamb have been a

partial answer to prayers. We recommend that you trust these men and listen to them. . . .

We pray that the God of Israel will use your tragic loss for good, and for destruction of the enemies of God and His people, just as He used the loss of His Son for the same. . . .

Randy, please help us to help you by cooperating with Col. Gritz so that further bloodshed can be avoided. Otherwise, we fear our actions and the death of your son could be in vain. We do not want his death to be just another evil and unnoticed sacrifice of Baal, and it will not be if we do it Yahweh's way. . . .

You have proven your point, now allow the God of Abraham, Isaac and Jacob to prove His. . . .

*Pete J. Peters*
*A leader in Christian Israel,*
*Pastor of the LaPorte Church*
*of Christ, and evangelistic leader*
*of Scriptures for America ministries*

When Gritz and Brown returned from meeting with Weaver, they brought with them a letter he had written. It offered the Weavers' version of what had happened and stated that the twenty-four-year-old Harris had killed Degan in self-defense. The letter also contained a surprise: "Samuel Hanson Weaver and Vicki Jean Weaver are Martyrs for Yah-Yahshua and the White Race."

It was the first time anyone among the lawmen knew that Vicki had been killed.

Two days later, on August 30, Harris surrendered to Gritz and McLamb. Suffering from a gunshot wound to the shoulder that had become infected and a collapsed lung, Harris was flown to a Spokane hospital where, after he was admitted, he was charged with the murder of Degan.

Later that same day, Weaver allowed Vicki's body to be removed.

The next day, August 31, Weaver diapered Elisheba, cradled her in his arms, and, with his two other daughters Sara and Rachel, surrendered to authorities. Like Harris, Weaver was charged with murder in the death of Degan.

The siege was over.

But for Identity Pastor Pete Peters the fight against injustice and tyranny had just started anew.

# The Seditionist

Pastor Pete Peters was angry. And he wanted his flock to know why.

Referring to the deaths of Vicki and Sam Weaver, Peters told listeners of his Scriptures for America Ministries, "Conspiracy reeks throughout this bloody murder on both the part of the media and the government. The media, on a national scale, gave little reporting on the murder of this white child and his white mother in comparison to [the attention given] the beating of the black man, Rodney King."

The deaths of Vicki and Sam Weaver did grab national headlines and stir the sympathy of some mainstream Americans. But not the majority of Americans. After all, didn't Weaver bring this tragedy down upon himself? Wasn't he a person who believed Jews were the children of Satan? Wasn't he a man wanted for selling sawed-off shotguns that he hoped would end up in the hands of street gangs? Wasn't a deputy marshal also killed? If not by Weaver, by his friend?

Once the siege ended and the story became back-page news, most Americans forgot the Weavers.

But not those Americans in the Patriot movement.

With about five million followers, it is a movement that exists at the fringe of American life and politics. On its moderate side are the John Birch Society and the conspiratorial segment of televangelist Pat Robertson's audience; both believe that a handful of wealthy elites are intent on establishing a one-world government or New World Order that will undermine Christianity. On the movement's more militant side are groups promoting themes of white supremacy and anti-Jewish bigotry—groups like the American Christian Patriots, Posse Comitatus, and Christian Identity. Somewhere in the middle is the Washington-based Liberty Lobby, which blends virulently anti-Zionist and racialist views with conspiracy theories and more orthodox conservative beliefs. Through its nationally circulated newspaper, *Spotlight*, the Lobby has served as a bridge between the two sides of the Patriot movement.

Some in the Patriot movement wish to live "off the grid"—no electricity, no sewage lines, no telephone—and as far from a population center as they can get. Some renounce all contacts with government—any form of government—by tearing up their driver's licenses, Social Security cards, marriage licenses, birth certificates, and hunting licenses. Some in the movement embrace racism and anti-Semitism. Some stockpile weapons and explosives and train themselves and their recruits in how to use them. Some believe the world is controlled by a Jewish cabal, or by the Trilateral Commission, the Council on Foreign Relations, or the United Nations, and that a New World Order will soon be imposed by any or all of these organizations.

There is, however, one thing they all hold in common: a relentless loathing and a deep hatred for the federal government. To those in the Patriot movement the siege at Ruby Ridge wasn't just an attempt to arrest one man. Rather, it was an attack on a way of life and the U.S. Constitution. It was a sign of just how far a federal government—no longer of the people, by the people, and for the people—would go to impose its tyranny upon freedom-loving Americans.

Such an act could not be allowed to slip from the public's consciousness.

"If anyone kills a person, the murderer shall be put to death at the evidence of witnesses," said Peters, quoting from Numbers. "[B]lood pollutes the land and no expiation can be made for the land for the blood that is shed . . . except by the blood of him who shed it."

Peters believed the event at Ruby Ridge could serve as a turning point for the Patriot movement. He was not alone in that belief.

"All of us in our groups . . . could not have done in the next twenty years what the federals did for our cause in eleven days in Naples, Idaho," said Chris Temple, a writer for *The Jubilee*, a major Christian Identity newspaper. "What we need to do is to not let this die and go away."

Instead, said Temple, the white supremacists should bury their differences and unite in their opposition to the federal government.

For more than twenty years, Peters and other believers in Christian Identity have tried to move the broader Patriot movement toward their more bigoted agenda. They met with some success in bringing most of the more radical groups, such as the Posse Comitatus, the Klan, and the Aryan Nations, under its theological tent. During that time Identity had grown from a sect with several hundred believers to one with tens of thousands of followers.

But while some progress had been made toward

unification, most groups under the Patriot movement umbrella fiercely maintained their independence from one another and often differed over tactics. As a result each group often saw the other as a potential adversary, not ally.

What happened at Ruby Ridge could change that.

Within days of Weaver's surrender to authorities, Peters sent personal letters to "a broad spectrum" of conservative writers, leaders, and ministers inviting them to the resort town of Estes Park, Colorado, for a conference that would "confront the injustice and tyranny manifested in the killings of Vicki Weaver and her son Samuel."

He even invited U.S. Attorney General William Barr to attend and explain the government's actions.

"Neither Samuel [n]or Vicki were wanted criminals, though Randy Weaver . . . had a warrant out for his arrest on an alleged misdemeanor weapons violation," wrote Peters. "Hardly a cause for the murder of a woman and a child and for the millions of dollars the government spent in its eighteen months of surveillance and apprehension of this family using a[n] FP-4 reconnaissance jet, U.S. Marshals, FBI agents, Bureau of Alcohol, Tobacco and Firearms (ATF) agents, Border Patrol, National Guard, local police, Sheriff's deputies, and Idaho State Police."

Barr declined the invitation.

So did many others.

Some couldn't afford to make the trip. Others said there was too little time to get prepared, since it was scheduled to start just sixty days after the siege ended. Others wanted to be assured adequate time to speak to the gathering. When informed no guarantees could be made until the start of the conference, they, too, declined to come. Some groups, such as the Rutherford Institute, a conservative think tank, said they wanted nothing to do with the meeting. Others didn't respond at all.

Still, 160 white, Christian men from thirty states said they would be there.

Among those who said they would attend was Louis Beam. He would give the keynote address. I'm sure that he never expected that our intelligence staff would obtain his speech.


Louis Beam was a man I knew all too well.

More than a decade earlier, Beam had actually challenged me to an old-fashioned duel. No seconds, no FBI agents, no judges. Just him and me. Man-to-man. My choice of weapons. Two of us walk into the woods, one walks out.

"If you are the base, despicable, low-down, vile poltroon I think you are, you will of course decline, in which case my original supposition will have been proven correct, and your lack of character verified," Beam wrote in a letter that arrived at my office by certified mail in January 1983. "If on the other hand you agree to meet me, you will raise immeasurably the esteem others hold you in. Imagine: Acquaintances, associates, supporters, friends, family—your mother— think of her, why I can just see her now, her heart just bursting with pride as you, for the first time in your life, exhibit the qualities of a man and march off to the field of honor. (Every mother has a right to be proud of her son once.) You will be worse than a coward if you deny her this most basic of rights. Think of her.

"In closing, let me make it clear that I believe you so base a coward that you will be too timid to even place a pen in hand and answer this letter, for I know a craven anti-Christ Jew when I have seen him. Here's your chance to prove me wrong."

Beam was not physically imposing. He stood about five feet seven inches, weighed around 130 pounds, and sported a BORN TO LOSE tattoo on his upper left forearm.

Still, he was not someone to be taken lightly.

As Grand Dragon of the Texas Knights of the Ku Klux Klan, Beam had formed a paramilitary wing called the Texas Emergency Reserve, composed mainly of ex–Vietnam War veterans. As many as 2,500 people were trained in hand-to-hand combat and guerrilla war tactics at the five secret camps Beam established throughout Texas. They were trained, Beam boasted, not only by ex-servicemen like himself—a highly decorated helicopter gunner in the Vietnam War—but also by active-duty military personnel from nearby bases such as Fort Hood, near Galveston. The camps were training people, he said, for the race war that was inevitable. It was a war he welcomed and looked forward to fighting.

Beam preached that the only race capable and fit to govern the United States was the white race. Never should a black man, a yellow man, or a brown man rule a white man. It was a point he often emphasized by wearing a tie that bore the word NEVER on it.

In Beam's view, the white race actually no longer ruled the United States. He believed a Jewish-led group of international conspirators, who used blacks, Hispanics, and other ethnic and religious minorities as pawns to do their bidding, now controlled the country. He also believed the conspirators were preparing to sacrifice all white, Christian Americans at the altar of a one-world government.

Beam looked forward to the day that open warfare would break out. He saw the resulting chaos as the perfect opportunity for him and the Texas Emergency Reserve to wrest control of the country from the conspirators and return it to the white, Christian majority.

"We intend to purge this land of every nonwhite person, idea, and influence," he vowed. "There should be no doubt that all means short of armed conflict have been exhausted."

Once the battle was joined and his enemies vanquished, Beam also had a plan for dealing with the conspirators in Texas. It was a plan he hoped supremacists in other states would follow.

"We'll set up our own state here [in Texas] and announce to all minorities that they have 24 hours to leave. Lots of them won't believe it or won't believe us when we say we'll get rid of them, so we'll have to exterminate a lot of them the first time around."

Beam was more than a man playing war games, roaming the woods in search of phantom enemies and shooting at paper targets with gross caricatures of African-Americans and Jews. He was more than hateful rhetoric. He also had a string of arrests for violent acts committed in the name of Christianity and "the American way." He was arrested when he allegedly tried to strangle Deng Xiaoping during the Chinese leader's visit to Houston, Texas, in 1980. Twice he was indicted—although the charges were later dropped—by state grand juries for blowing up buildings housing enemies of the right. One was a Communist Party headquarters; the other was a left-wing radio station. He also was charged with false imprisonment when he helped a white couple remove their daughter from a house she shared with a black man. That charge, too, was dropped.

Twice we had done battle with Beam, not in the woods, but in the courtroom. Twice we had won the day. There was no doubt in my mind those two embarrassing legal defeats in his own backyard of Texas were what motivated his challenge to me.

Our first encounter with Beam came in March 1981, after he had accepted a request from a renegade group of American fishermen to help them drive out the seventy-five or so Vietnamese immigrants and their families who were operating shrimp boats out of Galveston Bay. Beam saw this as the first skirmish in the race war he had long predicted would come. It would be to him what Lexington was to the American Patriots of 1776: the opening salvo to the start of an American Revolution.

As a means to his ends, Beam and members of his Klan militia—the Texas Emergency Reserve—mounted a terror campaign against the Vietnamese and the Americans who had befriended them. The campaign opened with the burning of an old shrimp boat with the words USS *Vietcong* painted on its hull as "an example" of what would happen if the Vietnamese entered Galveston Bay on May 15, 1981, the opening day of shrimping season. It continued with two crosses being burned, one on the yard of a Vietnamese fisherman, one near a marina—nicknamed Saigon Harbor—where several refugees docked their boats. Two more Vietnamese boats were later set afire. Telephone calls threatening arson and other reprisals were made against marina operators who rented dock space to the Vietnamese and merchants who did business with the refugees. Klan calling cards, warning that the Klan's next visit might be a "business call," appeared in the mailboxes of people who had befriended the Vietnamese. The cards were emblazoned with the image of a robed, hooded Klansman, mounted on a leaping horse and carrying a fiery torch.

The campaign climaxed with a group of the

American fishermen and fifteen Klan members boarding a shrimp boat—a mock human figure hanged in effigy on its riggings—for a show-of-force patrol around the bay. Some dressed in full Klan regalia, robes and hoods; others wore black Ku Klux Klan T-shirts; still others dressed in army fatigues. Most were armed with either shotguns or assault rifles that they brandished each time the boat stopped in front of the home of a Vietnamese fisherman or a dock where the immigrants worked on their boats. They concluded their patrol of the bay by firing a blank round from a cannon they had brought on board the ship. It shattered both the quiet of that March 15, 1981, morning, and, it seemed, the resolve of the Vietnamese fishermen.

We were just getting Klanwatch up and running when we read about the Klan's Galveston Bay "patrol" in the *New York Times*. While we knew the Klan had established a presence in Galveston Bay, it wasn't until we read about the harassment campaign that we felt we had an opportunity to take on Beam. But soon after we filed suit on behalf of the Vietnamese Fishermen's Association, we were informed by its leaders that their people were so frightened by the Klan's activities that they had decided against the legal action. The Vietnamese elders ordered the association members to sell their boats and give up fishing.

I was stunned, but I wasn't ready to accept defeat. I asked for a meeting with the association's elders. There, I apologized for the way they were being treated by my fellow Americans, outlined our legal strategy, and urged them to stand up to Beam and his bullies or face the all-too-real prospect of more harassment—not less—from the Klan. The elders reversed their decision, and we continued the lawsuit that sought an injunction against Beam and his men that would forbid them from interfering with the Vietnamese fishermen. On May 14, the day before the start of the shrimping season, a federal judge granted the injunction. The next morning, some of the other lawyers involved in the lawsuit and I watched as the Vietnamese blessed their fleet and entered Galveston Bay. I was never more proud to be a lawyer.

Still, it was a moment we couldn't savor for too long.

Although Beam and his Klan group were nowhere to be seen that morning, we knew they were still out there, waiting to intervene on behalf of the white majority in the next dispute that arose.

So we set out to put an end to the Texas Emergency Reserve.

At the time of our original lawsuit, we had filed an amended complaint that contended Beam's paramilitary camps violated a Texas state law that said other than the National Guard and the United States Armed Forces, no group of men were permitted to associate themselves in a military company. At the time of her ruling on the Vietnamese fishermen's case, the judge said there was not enough evidence to warrant a preliminary injunction stopping the Reserve from operating. She would resolve that issue at a trial at a later date. By the time we went to court to present the evidence we had collected on the Reserve, we were joined in our action by the Texas attorney general's office.

The evidence we presented included a series of videotapes of the Reserve in training that Beam had allowed a Rice University student to film. It was powerful, frightening material. In one segment, Beam, his face darkened by charcoal, instructed a dozen camouflaged fatigue-clad men on the purpose of an ambush. "When they get in the kill zone and you initiate fire," he said, "[inflict] maximum violence upon them. They mustn't have a chance to do anything but . . . die."

In another segment, Beam joked that his twice-a-month, weekend maneuvers were "a lot more fun than watching jungle bunnies run up and down [a basketball court] and toss balls."

After hearing the arguments and viewing the evidence, the judge, in June 1982, dismissed the Klan's contention that the training was defensive in nature and cited the March 15 boat ride as "the best illustration" of how the Klan used the Reserve to intimidate. She ordered the Texas Emergency Reserve disbanded.

Beam and the Reserve were out of the military business in Texas.

Unfortunately, Beam wasn't out of the hate business.

Following his defeat in the Vietnamese fishermen's case, Beam retreated north to the pine-scented mountains surrounding the small, one-time logging community of Hayden Lake, Idaho, where he joined up with the Reverend Richard Butler, a Hitler-worshiper and the patriarch of the militant right.

During the Vietnamese fishermen's case, Butler showed his support for Beam by traveling to Texas to speak at a rally and sit in on the trial for several days. When Beam came to him a beaten man, Butler welcomed him with open arms. Butler did not see a loser in Beam. Rather, he saw a bright, committed, and articulate Aryan warrior who was a skillful writer and good speaker. The perfect recruiter.

Soon after Beam arrived in Idaho, Butler named him Ambassador-at-Large for the Aryan Nations.

A workaholic, Beam divided his time between recruitment—he roamed the country and helped establish Aryan Nations chapters in Tennessee, Florida, Colorado, Texas, and Missouri—and writing. He coedited *The Inter-Klan Newsletter and Survival Alert*. Its typical fare included articles on military tactics, the creation of a cell structure for waging guerrilla war, and the "ten percent and out" solution—a proposal that called for a white nationalist state carved out of an area of the Pacific Northwest that equaled approximately 10 percent of the continental United States.

After joining Butler, Beam published *Essays of a Klansman*. One of the essays contained his assassination point system for racists wanting to attain the status of "Aryan Warrior." The system gave point values for eliminating certain types of people, from "street niggers" to race traitors to the U.S. president. The murder of a street cop was worth one-tenth of a point, for example, while the assassination of the president counted for a whole point, the amount needed to become an "Aryan Warrior." That system was later adopted by The Order, an Aryan Nations offshoot.

It was from Butler's Hayden Lake compound that Beam sent me his challenge to a duel. The letter was typed on Aryan Nations stationery.

By 1984, Beam discovered the newly laid information highway. He saw it as a route to thousands, maybe tens of thousands, of potential recruits. With Butler's blessing, Beam created the Aryan Nations Liberty Net, a system of nearly one dozen computer bulletin boards that carried their message of hate throughout the nation and allowed their followers to keep in touch with each other, as well as with members of other racist groups. Shortly after Beam took charge, the following thinly veiled message appeared: "According to the word of our God, Morris Dees has earned two death sentences. . . . Thy will be done on earth, as it is in heaven."

Beam's activities did not go unnoticed. Not by me or the federal government.

In what was dubbed Operation Clean Sweep, the federal government indicted Beam, Butler, Bob Miles—Grand Dragon of the Michigan Klan—and ten other racist leaders on the charge of seditious conspiracy. The indictment read:

"From on or about July 1983, and continuously thereafter, up to and including April 1985, in the Western District of Arkansas, and elsewhere, a group of persons willfully and knowingly combined, conspired, confederated and agreed together with each other to overthrow, put down and destroy by force the government of the United States and work for a new Aryan nation. . . ."

Acts the conspirators were charged with included firebombing a Jewish community center in Bloomington, Indiana, in August 1983; attempting to blow up a natural gas pipeline at Fulton, Arkansas, in November 1983; stealing more than $4 million from banks and armored cars in Seattle and Spokane, Washington, in 1983 and 1984; buying guns and explosives in Oklahoma and Missouri; and establishing a computer network to link right-wing groups nationwide.

The indictment also contended that Beam and the others planned to bomb federal buildings in Denver, Minneapolis, New Orleans, St. Louis, and Kansas City; poison water supplies in New York, Chicago, and Washington; sabotage railroads, utilities, and sewer lines; and assassinate federal judges. According to the government, Beam and his confederates intended to finance the plot through counterfeiting and additional bank and armored car robberies.

The indictments, which were issued in 1987, marked a major change in the way the government viewed the racist right. In the past, law enforcement had generally looked at it as a collection of isolated groups that shared the same hateful philosophy, but little else. Now it was seen as a single movement composed of different organizations that sometimes squabbled among themselves, sometimes competed, but more often collaborated. Along with Beam and Butler from Aryan Nations, and Miles from the Klan, others indicted included members of the Covenant, Sword and Arm of the Lord, and of The Order. And some of the prosecution's chief witnesses included racist leaders from the CSA, The Order, and the White Patriot Party, who claimed firsthand knowledge of the plot.

Soon after the indictments were handed up, Miles said a verdict would be either the crucifixion or the resurrection of the white supremacist movement. He predicted a crucifixion.

Beam didn't care to wait to find out which it would be. He fled to Mexico (he insisted he was on his honeymoon) and was placed on the FBI's Ten Most Wanted list. He was eventually captured by Mexican authorities, following a gun battle that left one Mexican policeman dead, and then returned to the United States for trial in Fort Smith, Arkansas.

Beam claimed the government offered him a reduced sentence and a "golf course country club, low-security prison if I would turn on Pastor Butler and Bob Miles. They also offered me my wife [who was imprisoned in Mexico in connection with the shooting death of the policeman].

"I said no, for I still believe in those concepts of honor, duty, loyalty, and courage."

During the trial, the government presented more than 1,200 pieces of evidence and testimony from more than 100 witnesses. James Ellison, the leader of the Covenant, Sword and Arm of the Lord, said the plot to overthrow the government was hatched during the 1983 Aryan

World Congress. All the participants at the meeting signed a statement and then announced, said Ellison, that what they were doing was a "conspiracy of treason."

At the same meeting, said Ellison, participants were so embittered by the death of Identity adherent and Posse Comitatus member Gordon Kahl that a list was drawn up of people who should be killed in revenge. The list included David Rockefeller, Norman Lear, and Henry Kissinger.

According to the affidavits of two members of The Order, the more than $4 million netted from the armored car heists were split among white supremacist leaders to help finance the plot. Those who received money included Tom Metzger, leader of the White Aryan Resistance, $260,000 to $300,000; Glenn Miller, leader of the White Patriot Party, $200,000; Louis Beam, $100,000; Robert Mathews, head of The Order, $100,000; Richard Butler, $40,000; and Bob Miles, $15,500. The affidavits also stated William Pierce, leader of the National Alliance, received $50,000 in recognition of his authorship of *The Turner Diaries*, a fictional account of a race war leading to the overthrow of the government. The Order had used the book as a blueprint for its crime spree in the Northwest.

Still a third member of The Order, Zillah Craig, testified she helped distribute the money.

Except for Glenn Miller, the defendants—and the others named in the affidavits—all denied receiving any money. The defendants—some serving as their own attorneys—argued there was no plot to overthrow the government. They were only exercising their constitutional right to freedom of speech, they said. The attorney for Bob Miles, Deday LaRene, acknowledged his client was a "bit of a cheerleader for the right wing," but insisted the government must prove that Miles and the others had "crossed the line from advocating . . . a position . . . to a criminal plot."

After a seven-week trial and twenty hours of deliberation, the all-white jury agreed in April 1988 that the government hadn't proved the defendants "crossed the line." Beam, Butler, Miles, and the others were acquitted. (Perhaps indicative of the jury's true sentiments was the fact that during the trial, two of the female jurors fell in love with two of the defendants—one of the relationships flowered into marriage. A third juror, a man, gave an interview after the verdict in which he expressed antiblack opinions similar to those held by the defendants.)

No one seemed more surprised by the acquittals than Bob Miles, who had served time in prison for bombing school buses that were to be used to integrate Michigan school districts. Instead of celebrating the resurrection of the radical right, Miles responded to a question about the movement's future by saying: "Who knows? What movement? What's left of it?"

Beam, however, seized the limelight following the verdicts. During an impromptu speech on the steps of the courthouse, he claimed victory over ZOG and vowed to continue the fight against it "til we get this country back."

A little while later, Beam traveled to Pulaski, Tennessee, where he spoke to a gathering of skinheads, Klansmen, and Christian Patriots.

"They call me a seditionist," he said. "If you look at the definition of seditionist, it's one who opposes the established authority.

"And I am a seditionist," he shouted.

He then promised the group they were going to have America back, and that "No one will have it if we can't have it. Hail Victory! White Victory!"

His words and actions in the weeks following the trial dispelled the wishful thoughts some people had that the trial would scare Beam into private life and away from white supremacist activities. Still, when Beam returned to Texas he maintained a much lower profile. "I went home to a small community . . . where I raised black-eyed peas and blond-headed kids," he said.

He did a bit more than that.

Beam busied himself with his computer network, editing and publishing his newsletter, now called *The Seditionist*, and refining his thoughts on cell structures for guerrilla warfare. These ideas eventually became the foundation for an essay entitled "Leaderless Resistance."

Then came the siege at Ruby Ridge.

"The attack on the Weaver family by federal assassins was an attack upon every family in the United States," Beam told the Estes Park gathering. "This time the federal terrorists, masquerading as officers, came for Randy Weaver. Next time they may come for you. So I went because they may also come again for me.

"If federal terrorism goes unchallenged, then no one in this nation is safe. Government terrorism, if ignored, does not go away, but gets worse. Like a lion having tasted the blood of human victims, they will come for more, new victims."

It was vintage Beam. He wanted to let the world—especially the racist world—know he was back.

Once more, Beam uprooted himself from Texas and moved to Idaho, where he reunited with Butler and the Aryan Nations. To provide support for Randy Weaver and what remained of his family, Beam lent his prestige to United Citizens for Justice, a group formed by Chris Temple, a contributor to *The Jubilee*, and John Trochmann, who would later establish the Militia of Montana.

He also vowed to avenge the deaths of Vicki and Sam Weaver.

"This is your country, your government, your police state. America, love it or die," he mocked. "Those in government who have labored over the years to build the road that leads to a new world order . . . are besides themselves with joy, excitement, and anticipation for they are almost there. A short, short distance remains, and their objective will have been reached.

"Ah, but those last few miles will be rough ones," Beam warned. "For in the name of Yahweh . . . we pledge that those last few miles will not just be paved with the bones, blood, and broken hearts of patriots. We will pave that road with tyrants' blood, tyrants' bones, and you shall know the broken heart."

Beam can play the buffoon, as his often bloated rhetoric and his ridiculous challenge to me demonstrated. But it would be foolish for anyone to dismiss him as a harmless ideologue. There is nothing harmless about Louis Beam. Charismatic, intelligent, and well spoken, Beam moves people. He gets them to embrace his hateful ideas, to follow him, and, in some cases, as he did in Texas, to join his own personal army and to act on those ideas. He was, and is, far and away the most dangerous—and most radical—of the racist leaders.

Even before David Duke was elected to the Louisiana legislature in 1989 and won a majority of the white votes in the state in his losing races for the U.S. Senate in 1990 and the governorship in 1991, voters across the nation—disenchanted with incumbents—were being influenced by antigovernment appeals. Racist messages lurked just below the surface in sound-bite ads attacking crime, welfare cheats, and affirmative action. And those messages worked. Mean-spirited radio talk show hosts added a daily layer of negative government feelings to a growing and receptive audience.

If antigovernment appeals were moving angry but otherwise rational voters, it was no surprise when Beam hit pay dirt with his audience at the Estes Park conference. Those who came to hear him and people like Pete Peters truly believed that elected officials, from local to federal, had become tools of a "one-world government" aimed at enslaving them and the rest of America.

# Rocky Mountain Rendezvous

They began arriving at Estes Park on Thursday, October 22, 1992. They came separately, and in pairs and threesomes. They came in cars, pickup trucks, and vans. Some flew in for the event that would come to be known as the Rocky Mountain Rendezvous.

It was a true cross-section of the far-right movement.

There was Louis Beam, of course, who came down from Idaho. So did Richard Butler, the founder of the Aryan Nations, and Tom Stetson, the leader of the Concerned Citizens of Idaho, the American Christian Patriots, and the Sovereign Citizens of America Network.

Red Beckman, longtime tax protester and leader of the so-called fully informed jury movement, came from Montana, as did *Jubilee* writer Chris Temple. *The Jubilee*'s publisher, Paul Hall, was there from California, and Larry Pratt, founder of Gun Owners of America, came in from Virginia. Identity leader Charles Weisman of Minnesota was there. So, too, was Earl Jones, head of the Christian Crusade for Truth, who came up from New Mexico. Christian Identity minister James Bruggeman arrived from North Carolina, as did attorney Kirk Lyons, who had boasted that the number one priority of his CAUSE Foundation, an organization that offers legal support to extremist organizations, was to "sue the federal government back to the Stone Age." (CAUSE stands for Canada, Australia, United States, South Africa, and Europe—everywhere that "kindred" white people are found.)

Identity adherents Doug Evers of Wisconsin, John Nelson of Colorado, and Doug Pue of Arizona, also came. As did Beam's colleague John Trochmann and Trochmann's nephew Randy, who drove in from Montana.

The meeting was really extraordinary. It managed to bring together various factions of the hard extremist right into a kind of tacit agreement.

That fact was not lost on those who attended the Rendezvous.

"Men came together who in the past would normally not be caught together under the same roof, who greatly disagree with each other on many theological and philosophical points, whose teachings contradict each other in many ways," said Peters. "Yet, not only did they come together, they worked together for they all agreed what was done to the Weaver family was wrong and could not, and should not, be ignored by Christian men."

"The federals have by their murder of Samuel and Vicki Weaver brought us all together under the same roof for the same reason," Beam said. Gone was the factional infighting that had characterized so many far-right gatherings in the past, he noted. "The two murders of the Weaver family have shown all of us that our religious, our political, our ideological differences mean nothing to those who wish to make us all slaves. We are viewed by the government as the same, the enemies of the state.

"When they come for you, the federals will not ask if you are a Constitutionalist, a Baptist, Church of Christ, Identity Covenant believer, Klansman, Nazi, home schooler, Freeman New Testament believer, [or] fundamentalist. . . . Those who wear badges, black boots, and carry automatic weapons, and kick in doors already know all they need to know about you. You are enemies of the state."

Those drawn together over the Weaver incident, Peters said, were "brave men . . . who did not fear potential unjust associations that could be made by the lawless anti-Christ media in our land. Nor did they fear potential police state spying eyes or possible unjust charges by any government official or attorney general."

Although they constituted a majority of those in attendance, it wasn't only a meeting of far-right revolutionaries and Identity believers.

Baptists, Presbyterians, members of the Church of Christ, and Mennonites also attended the Rendezvous.

"If you want to know what my doctrine is, it's Mennonite," Kansas attorney Steve Graber told the conclave's participants. "And I've not come because of your doctrine or my doctrine. I came here . . . because I'm very interested in knowing what the facts are.

"How about let's just forget what your religion is. How about let's talk about the truth. How about let's talk about what the evidence is. How about let's quit playing these silly games and discarding somebody because we may not agree with their doctrine," said Graber, who, during the siege at Ruby Ridge, was contacted by some of Weaver's supporters and asked to handle the case. (Soon after Weaver's surrender, Wyoming attorney Gerry Spence agreed to defend him; Graber was not involved in the case.)

A onetime national staff member of the Rutherford Institute, a think tank and law center that provides legal support for an array of right-wing causes, Graber was one of two visible links to the mainstream New Right.

The second—and probably most intriguing—link between those who would be comfortable inside the Washington beltway and those who inhabit the extreme reaches of contemporary American fanaticism was Larry Pratt.


A slightly built, bespectacled man, Pratt is the executive director of both Gun Owners of America and the Committee to Protect the Family Foundation, an organization that raises funds for antiabortion extremist Randall Terry. He also founded English First, a 250,000-member group that sponsors efforts to block bilingual education.

A former Virginia legislator, Pratt moves easily through the corridors of power. His political action committee has doled out thousands of dollars to several dozen conservative Republican candidates, including Maryland representative Roscoe Bartlett and Texas congressman Richard Armey. Pratt told those gathered at Estes Park that if Armey "becomes the Republican leader, we will have the opportunity, we will have the possibility of having some issues fought."

As comfortable as he is among those inside the beltway, Pratt is equally at home with individuals who prefer combat boots to Guccis, camouflage uniforms to three-piece, tailored suits, and the practice of guerrilla warfare tactics to the playing of politics. As a result, he frequently serves as a bridge between the two groups—the main-stream politicians, at both the federal and state levels, and far-right elements—by bringing them together at fund-raisers, dinners, and other social events.

At Estes Park, Pratt damned his competition—the National Rifle Association—with faint praise. "You know, these are the guys defending the Second Amendment," he said.

"They've done some wonderful historical research and they've done some excellent comparative analysis of gun laws in other countries and how they don't work and many other things like that. Much information is available from them. But not wisdom, not discernment."

The problem, said Pratt, whose Gun Owners of America claimed 130,000 members, was with the NRA's traditional lobbying techniques. An NRA representative would "go and offer technical criticism of the bill. . . . And the legislators' say, 'Well, fine, no problem, we'll just write that into the bill, too.'

"They [legislators] can say what if we solve this problem, that problem, the other problem, then will you support the bill? And you're sunk. They could even make the bill worse."

The way to avoid that problem, Pratt explained, was to have people like Bartlett and Armey in leadership roles in Congress to "articulate our position, to join the debate, to force the other side to explain why we shouldn't be able to have firearms to defend ourselves since the police can't do it." The country needed people who understood that the right to bear arms was not an issue that could be bargained away in some backroom deal to get a bill passed.

"We have a lot of confusion in our land, and the bottom line is that it is a spiritual battle. This is not a political issue. This is something that comes first and foremost from the Scripture. What I see in Scripture is not that we have a right to keep and bear arms, but that we have a responsibility to do so," said Pratt. "For a man to refuse to provide adequately for his and his family's defense would be to defy God."

The one sure way to guarantee that responsibility is not taken from a person—especially by the government—is through the formation of "recognized, but unorganized, militias" that are not provided for or commanded by the governor of the state or the legislature.

"The history of the United States for years before and after the founding of the Republic was the history of an armed people with functioning militias involved in civil defense (or police work, if you will)," Pratt wrote in his book *Armed People Victorious*, published in 1990. "While the United States has forgotten its success in this area, other countries have rediscovered them. It is time that the United States return to reliance on an armed people. There is no acceptable alternative."

Ever since the publication of his book, which glorified the role vigilante groups played in Guatemala and the Philippines, Pratt had become—to some—the father of the modern militia movement. At Estes Park, he had an attentive audience.

To Pratt, armed citizen militias would cure many of the ills facing the country. The militias could be used to win the war on drugs and to end the flood of illegal immigrants into the country. They also would deter riots, such as the one that rocked Los Angeles following the verdicts in the Rodney King beating case. The Los Angeles riot, Pratt told the gathering, was a "great lesson in self-defense . . . and the importance of having an armed militia to organize quickly and effectively to defend people in their homes and in their stores and their livelihoods."

Citizen militias, he predicted, could stop future Ruby Ridges from happening.

"One can only speculate that had there been an effective militia in Naples, Idaho, which could have been mobilized after the U.S. Marshal murdered Sammy Weaver by shooting him in the back . . . [i]t is entirely possible that Vicki Weaver would not have been murdered later on by an FBI-trained assassin while she was holding a baby in her arms," he wrote in an essay that appeared in *Safeguarding Liberty, the Constitution & Citizen Militias*, a book he edited.

The Rocky Mountain Rendezvous was called, as Pete Peters noted in his opening remarks, to confront the injustice and tyranny manifested in the killings of Vicki Weaver and her son, Samuel, and to decide "what to do about it."

And no one spoke to that issue more eloquently than Louis Beam.

"Randy Weaver's baby cries out for its mama. We, the people, cry out for justice. Randy Weaver's baby cries out for its mama. We cry out for truth. The cries of baby Elisheba will forever go unanswered. But in the name of all that is holy, all that is good, and all that is just in this country . . . our cry for justice will not be ignored. Let those who are honest and good in this country join with us. Let those who harbor secret crimes in their heart and who wish to shield the guilty scurry for the holes of darkness. We bear the torch of light, of justice, of liberty, and we will be heard.

"We will not yield this country to the forces of darkness, oppression, and tyranny," vowed Beam.

He also warned his audience that the Weaver family

would not be the last to experience the tender mercies of a government gone mad.

"The federals went after Randy Weaver as an object lesson to each of us here," he said. "That lesson: oppose the government and you and your family will suffer. Of course, we as Christians have no choice in the matter. For if we do not oppose the government now, while we still can, . . . we will suffer more. For it is the enemies of Christ that we wage our struggle against, and there are no bounds to their evil. There are no limits to their lust for power."

The amens, hallelujahs, and applause that erupted from the audience made Beam's closing words almost inaudible.

"I cannot compromise with such men for they are without principle. I cannot reason with such men; they are men without reason," he said. "But I can warn them, and it is a warning they must take to heart. I and many others in this country, many in this room tonight, will not roll over and play dead for your New World Order."

Peters also shared with the participants the letter he had written to Randy Weaver during the siege at Bo Gritz's request. Peters knew Gritz well. Gritz was a frequent speaker at Peters's annual Scriptures for America Family Bible Camp, and Peters had financed his book, *Called to Serve*. The book claims that "eight Jewish families virtually control the entire Federal Reserve Board."

After reading his letter, Peters acknowledged he had had second thoughts about sending it along through Gritz. "In fact, I've had pangs of guilt wondering if I should have even written the letter," he admitted. "If I should have encouraged him to come down off the mountain."

He noted that there were some men in the audience

who believed anyone caught in a situation similar to Weaver's should seriously weigh the consequences of surrender and should recognize that, in some instances, death may be preferable and more beneficial than coming down off the mountain.

His pangs of guilt disappeared soon after Weaver called him from prison. "I asked [Randy] specifically, because I had to know, do you regret having come down the mountain or do you wish you had stayed there," Peters recounted. "I'm pleased to report to you . . . he said he was thankful he came down off the mountain because, otherwise, [the three] daughters in his family would be dead."

Peters also shared a letter he had received from Weaver's sixteen-year-old daughter Sara, just a couple of days before the start of the meeting at Estes Park. That letter read:

> To all of my brothers and sisters who have cared enough to help us out with support and love.
>
> Words cannot express my appreciation. You have all been so wonderful to us. I could never repay you.
>
> These terrible things that have happened, have been very hard on all of us, but I know it's led a lot of people to the truth. And that is all mom and Sam would ask for. Our creator, Yahweh-Yahshua Messiah, his will I won't question. . . .
>
> I guess I just wish to thank-you all from the bottom of my heart.
>
> May Yahweh Bless and Guide you.
>
> *Love,*
> *Sara Weaver*
> *and family*

While there was much talk about the Weavers and hand-wringing over what happened to them, the incident was only the "calling," the hook on which many other agendas were hung. Men like Peters saw the botched arrest attempt against Randy Weaver as the perfect rallying cry for militant elements of the far right, as a way to galvanize extremists throughout the country. "There is a host of Christian soldiers . . . that are willing and able to do something but they don't know what to do," he told the assembly. "If given a direction, a powerful force could be tapped, harnessed, and used for the establishment of a Christian civil body politic for carrying out the judgments of God."

Among those judgments, said Peters, was forcing the federal government to "study and apply the teachings of the Holy Scriptures," much as Islamic fundamentalists seek to impose their version of the Koran upon an unholy world of nonbelievers.

Men like Peters also saw the Weaver case as a way to rekindle the debate that began in the 1850s and ended, many people thought, with the Civil War over the legitimacy of the federal government.

All the angry rhetoric at the Rendezvous flowed in one direction—at the federal government. Not the Jews, not the blacks, not the homosexuals, not the abortionists, although each group was tagged throughout the three days. The enemy was defined clearly as the federal government and the New World Order.

They had learned an important lesson. At no time during the conference did Louis Beam talk about "White America" or rail against the "anti-Christ Jew devils." None of the speakers publicly used "nigger," "race traitor," or "mud people," words and phrases that were commonplace at earlier Klan rallies and Aryan Nations gatherings.

They were smart this time. They borrowed a page out of David Duke's book.

Duke had long been the most widely known white supremacist in the country. As a college student at Louisiana State University he picketed a speech by liberal lawyer William Kunstler in 1970 wearing a storm trooper uniform and carrying a sign bearing the message GAS THE CHICAGO 7. Later, he became the Imperial Wizard of the Knights of the Ku Klux Klan. In 1980, he broke with the Klan and formed the National Association for the Advancement of White People, combining mainstream conservative opposition to welfare, affirmative action, and forced school busing with white supremacy. At that time he also published a plan calling for separate territorial enclaves for blacks, Jews, and whites—including the removal of Louisiana's Cajun population to Canada. (A similar plan was later adopted by the Aryan Nations in 1986.)

Then, in the latter part of the 1980s, Duke claimed he had undergone a Christian awakening, publicly disavowed his racist roots, professed a desire to work within the system, and announced his candidacy for president of the United States. His running mate on the Populist Party ticket was Col. Bo Gritz, who would later withdraw to run for a Nevada congressional seat.

While on the campaign trail, Duke refrained from the public use of racial slurs, but his themes resonated along racial lines. He employed many of the same coded symbols—affirmative action, welfare, and crime—that some Republican candidates have used to arouse racist fears in white voters. Duke turned concern for the declining living standards of white workers into attacks on affirmative action; he blamed low wage rates on immigrant labor; he wanted to throw the lazy off welfare rolls. He cast himself as a white civil rights activist.

"White people don't have rights in this country any-more," he said. "White people today are the victims of greater racial discrimination than blacks faced anytime in the last one hundred years."

Despite his efforts to distance himself from his racist past, Duke had a hard time concealing all the evidence of his true feelings. At his campaign headquarters in Metairie, Louisiana, a person could purchase Nazi and racist books and pamphlets that outlined alleged biological evidence that blacks were mentally inferior to whites, warned of the power of the Zionist-controlled media, and contended the Holocaust never occurred.

Nonetheless, his move away from an overt racist agenda paid dividends.

In 1988, Duke garnered more than 23,000 votes as the Populist Party candidate in Louisiana's presidential primary, outpolling two mainstream candidates, Arizona governor Bruce Babbitt and Illinois senator Paul Simon. On the Super Tuesday ballot in Arkansas, Missouri, Oklahoma, and Texas, Duke received more than 41,000 votes. In February 1989, running as a Republican, Duke won a seat as a representative in the Louisiana legislature. Prior to his election, Duke said that winning the race "would be a springboard to turning back the tide toward the White majority in the country" and "could break the dike and set loose a flood of white activism and political involvement."

Then, in the fall of 1990, he drew 44 percent of the vote against incumbent U.S. Senator J. Bennett Johnston in the general election. A solid majority of the white voters in Louisiana cast their ballots in his favor.

Duke's success did not go unnoticed by others in the racist right.

Even Louis Beam saw lots of nonviolent opportunities in a political climate overheated by such explosive

issues as welfare reform, immigration, and the widen-
ing chasm between the haves and the have-nots.

"We still have the power to take back America so
long as free elections are held," he wrote in an essay
that appeared in *The Jubilee*. "[W]e must all arm ourselves with a voter registration slip and use it like a .308
sniper weapon to 'take out' the infectious bought
whores of the new world government who are now
proposing to rule us all with an Orwellian iron fist—forever beating us all into submission, while claiming to
protect us."

Duke was invited to attend the Rendezvous, but to
Peters's dismay he never "acknowledged . . . or responded"
to the many telephone requests or the letter that was sent.

Still, his strategy was at work at the event. Those in
attendance were careful not to use white supremacist and
neo-Nazi labels. Instead, they repeatedly referred to
themselves as "just good Christians" or the "elders of
Zion" who have all "come together as the Body of Christ."
They also refrained, publicly at least, from using racial
and anti-Semitic slurs and epithets. They referred to their
enemies as "evil doers," "sodomites," and "federals."

They even decried "certain media sources and government entities" that insisted on labeling them and the
Weavers as white separatists or white supremacists. "It
needs to be determined who is doing this and by what
authority," complained one conference-goer. "It appears
such terms are being used by a New World Order crowd
with the definition being 'terrorists of the New World
Order.'"

"The current situation in America is one in which the
established government does not punish the evil-doers,
but rather is increasingly using its power to punish the
righteous," argued Peters. "It is a tyrannical government."

That theme was rapped out again and again as different "pastors" and "patriots" took the podium for one hour each.

Red Beckman condemned the federal income tax; Earl Jones reported on the construction of concentration camps; Charles Weisman related the parallels between today's movement and the "first" American Revolution; Richard Butler lambasted the news media; Doug Evers addressed government police state tactics in the health care field; Doug Pue revealed how the movement's children were being targeted through inoculations; John Nelson examined the one-world government, Interpol, and how Americans were losing their birthright; Reily Donica of Oklahoma sermonized on why a person must learn to pray and hold a gun; Greg Dixon of Indiana proffered "The Theology of Christian Resistance"; Del Knudson of Washington related his family's experience at the hands of the Bureau of Alcohol, Tobacco, and Firearms; and S. A. Freeman, also of Washington, told of what Christian citizens were doing to stop police brutality.

Events since the Rendezvous show that quite a bit more than talk was produced at the three-day strategy session. The ground had been prepared years before, but the Estes Park meeting actually established a working structure for the current militia/Christian Patriot movement.

That structure was hammered out by a number of committees established during the conference. Among those panels were the Divine Ways and Means Committee, which outlined the biblical laws that had been violated by the New World Order and the vigilante action—"in conformity with Biblical precedence and directives"—needed to punish the "evil doers"; the Sacred Warfare Action Tactics (SWAT) Committee, which evaluated "what our people would be forced to consider should tyranny and despotism become the order of the day and no other recourse is available"; and the Legal and Lawful Affairs Committee, which considered the legal initiatives that must be taken in order to fight a corrupt system of justice.

"Because of the diversity of views of the men involved, unanimous agreement with each and every sentence in the committee reports was not possible," acknowledged Peters on the final day of the gathering as he introduced each committee representative. "[But] the committee reports contain a general consensus of each [panel's] view."

Some of the reports had been deliberately kept vague, admitted Earl Jones, because "we wanted to get this information published" without the government coming "down with conspiracy charges on the whole bunch of us."

One report in particular that had been kept vague was that from Jones's SWAT committee, a group comprised of a "bunch of young bulls" who were "upset . . . mad . . . angry at the tyrannical government," according to Jones. He said they came on to the committee wanting to establish standard operating procedures for dealing with future confrontations between movement members and the government. And they brought with them more information than is found in a "Special Forces manual," Jones added.

But none of that information had reached the final report. "We don't want to give the impression of breaking any laws of any sort," said Jones.

Still, the reports endorsed by the general assembly of the Rendezvous made clear the direction in which the participants wanted to go.

The group embraced the "concept of church militias, which were common with our Christian forefathers in the 17th and 18th centuries." They contended an unorganized militia—defined by Larry Pratt as "one not being provided for or commanded by the governor of the state or the legislature"—was both an individual's right and the one true line of defense against a government bent on taking away all rights of the individual. They endorsed Louis Beam's strategy for organizing militia units around the revolutionary tactic of "leaderless resistance," a strategy that calls for autonomous cells, comprised of no more than eight to ten members, organized around ideology, not leaders.

The attendees at the Rendezvous also supported a series of initiatives designed to return the justice system to the American people.

"Corruption and decline is the hallmark of America's judicial system, and justice is a very rare commodity," said North Carolina attorney Kirk Lyons, a member of the Legal and Lawful Affairs panel. "The best chance for justice in the courts comes from the power vested in an informed jury and grand jury. Only by interposing the conscience of the Christian community between the defendant in a criminal case and the power of the government can a fair trial be expected; especially where the defendant is politically and theologically incorrect."

To educate potential jurors, the committee called for distributing copies of the *Citizen's Rule Book* throughout the country and using the book as a basis for jury rights seminars.

Long circulated in the Christian Patriot movement, the *Citizen's Rule Book* contends that juries do not have to listen to judges who tell them they must apply the law whether they approve of it or not. Instead, the book maintains, a citizen has the power, as well as both the right and obligation, to check abuses by government and fight bad laws by vetoing wrongful prosecutions.

The book also says juries have the right to raise questions about the legality of some constitutional amendments. In particular, it claims that there is a "great deal" of suspicion about whether the Thirteenth Amendment, which ended slavery, the Fourteenth Amendment, which extended citizenship rights to the newly freed slaves, and the Sixteenth Amendment, which imposed the income tax, are legally in effect.

"[I]nstructing people on the power of the jury is the best safeguard we have for justice left because we can't count on the judges. We can't count on the lawyers," said Lyons. "All we can count on is our Heavenly Father and his spirit going through some honest jurors."

In the coming months that message would find its way into the jury box, first at the trial of Randy Weaver and, later, at the murder trial of eleven Branch Davidians. In both cases, jurors were mailed "Jury Power" kits that told them they didn't have any obligation to follow the judge's legal instructions or to convict the defendants. The mailings caught almost everyone by surprise since the judges in both cases had assured the jurors that their identities wouldn't be revealed. But supporters of the Fully Informed Jury Association, the organization that mailed the kits, had followed the jurors to their secret parking lots and jotted down their license plate numbers.

Finally, those who gathered at Estes Park agreed to send an open letter to the Weaver family. It read:

> Impelled by the spirit of our HEAVENLY
> FATHER, and hearing the cry of innocent blood
> shed in the land, WE, 160 Christian men assembled
> for three days of prayer and counsel, at Estes Park,
> Colorado.

At our gathering the sad events of Ruby Creek [*sic*] were recounted.

We have not the words to write nor mouths to speak that can adequately express the sorrow and the righteous indignation we feel at your tragic loss.

We have not the power to restore to you the loved ones who were cruelly stolen from you!

But as Christian men, led by the word of our Heavenly Father, we are determined to never rest while you are in peril and distress!

We are determined to employ HIS strength and to work continually to insure that Vicki and Samuel's mortal sacrifices were not in vain!

We call for Divine Judgment upon the wicked and the guilty who shed the blood of Vicki and Samuel!

We are committed to standing by you, the living, in your hour of trial!

We are committed to keeping you continually in our prayers and to do all in our physical and spiritual power to relieve your distress. Furthermore, we are committed to seeking justice for you and your slain loved ones on behalf of all Christians of goodwill. AMEN.

At the conclusion of the conclave, it was clear those in attendance were feeling good about themselves and the movement's future.

"The world today sees a ragtag band that they would mock. Their laughter does not bother me," concluded Peters. "[T]hey may chide us and they may think they have the power in their riches, in their accumulated media. [But] may we leave this assembly knowing who has the greater power."

Pastor Charles Weisman of Minnesota, who chaired the Divine Ways and Means Committee, proclaimed in a similar vein, "[W]e are in the process of growing into a Christian civil body politic. We're at an immature state right now, but we're in that process, growing into it . . . taking dominion once again. [W]hen the body is mature enough, we will be ready to punish all disobedience."

At Estes Park, the movement changed from a disparate, fragmented group of pesky—and at times dangerous—gadflies to a serious, armed political challenge to the state itself.

During that weekend in the Rockies, a network of militant antigovernment zealots was created. Alliances were formed from diverse factions: Identity, Posse Comitatus, the Klan, Aryan Nations, reconstructionists and other fundamentalist Christians, neo-Nazis, tax resisters, Second Amendment advocates, and antiabortion extremists.

The Rocky Mountain Rendezvous that was held in tranquil Estes Park, Colorado, was a watershed for the racist right. Whether they knew that at the time doesn't matter. They know it now.

# Waco and Guns

Ruby Ridge ignited the militia movement.

It was the impetus for Estes Park, from which Louis Beam, Pete Peters, Kirk Lyons, and the rest took away a unified strategy for battling a government with which they saw themselves at war. When they returned to their home states, they shared that strategy with their friends, neighbors, and others who, like them, felt frustrated by too many regulations, threatened by a one-world economy, and frightened by a government that had gotten too big and too powerful.

They also took it with them on the road to gun shows and Preparedness Expos—events held in civic centers and convention halls from Miami to Missoula—where America's mainstream often meets its fringe cousins.

There, amid tables laden with Ruger Mini-14 semi-automatic rifles, Mossberg shotguns, and Beretta 9mm pistols, and piled high with holsters, military ponchos, and camouflage uniforms, they peddled the idea of militias as a defense against a tyrannical government, as a way to prevent any more Ruby Ridges.

They met with limited success. In many instances, they simply found themselves preaching to the choir, fellow members of the Patriot movement.

Then, some six months later, the spark that was Ruby Ridge was fanned into a flame seven miles northeast of Waco, Texas. More than one hundred agents of the Bureau of Alcohol, Tobacco, and Firearms leapt from the back of cattle trailers and stormed the compound of the Branch Davidians—part religious cult, part paramilitary group—to arrest its thirty-three-year-old leader David Koresh. The arrest attempt was a disaster. Although the ATF was informed it had lost the element of surprise, it proceeded with the raid anyway. A hail of gunfire left four ATF agents dead and sixteen other law enforcement officers wounded. A two-year-old daughter of Koresh and five other Davidians also were killed in the exchange. After the agents retreated, the government laid siege to the compound, saying it was prepared to stay and, eventually, negotiate for as long as it took to avoid further bloodshed. Through its negotiations, the FBI won the release of twenty children and adults from the compound.

During the negotiations, the nascent militia movement rallied to the defense of the Branch Davidians. Louis Beam traveled to Waco to cover the incident for *The Jubilee*. At one of the daily press briefings, he got into a shouting match with FBI agents over the conduct of the ATF's initial raid. The confrontation soon escalated into a shoving contest, and Beam was arrested. The charges were eventually dropped.

Linda Thompson, founder of the Indianapolis-based Unorganzied Militia of the United States of America, called supporters to the police barricades surrounding the compound. Dressed in a camouflage uniform, Thompson brandished an unloaded AR-15 and demanded the government end the siege.

Kirk Lyons, the North Carolina attorney who specializes in white supremacist causes, also was on the scene. "We were a little behind the power curve on Randy Weaver," Lyons explained, "but we were determined not to make the same mistake twice."

By the fourth day of the siege, Lyons and his CAUSE Foundation were in Waco. "Our purpose was to start building a defense team that could support and defend these people," he said. "The government was distorting their message and image and what actually happened there."

Perhaps because he was curious about how the Southern Poverty Law Center would react, or perhaps because he wanted to place us on the wrong side of history, Lyons tried to enlist us as part of his defense team. During the siege, he called our office and asked if we would help him file habeas corpus actions on behalf of the Davidians. A habeas corpus action is a legal proceeding to determine whether someone in government custody is being lawfully detained. Most habeas actions are filed on behalf of prisoners who claim that their criminal trials were unfair. Lyons's apparent theory was that the government's siege amounted to the illegal imprisonment of the Davidians in the compound.

We politely declined Lyons's invitation to join him in Waco. Although we were concerned that the siege might end in bloodshed, we thought that the best way to defuse the situation was to have the Davidians come out of their compound, not to file lawsuits for them. And, of course, we would never have worked directly with Lyons. The fact that he had represented Louis Beam was not really what bothered us. Lawyers are often called upon to represent those with whom they disagree. Gerry Spence's defense of Randy Weaver is a good example of that noble tradition. What bothered us was that Lyons was not just Beam's lawyer, he was his comrade.

Lyons proceeded without us.

"We . . . filed a historic . . . temporary restraining order asking the judge to order the feds to pull back and not kill everyone, so that peaceful negotiations could begin," said Lyons. "The judge dismissed it. He didn't rise to the level that we thought he should and order the feds back."

Perhaps it would have been better for everyone had the court acted despite the absence of a legal basis for doing so.

On April 19, 1993, the FBI, citing concerns for the safety of the children inside the compound, ended the fifty-one days of negotiations and mounted a second raid. It culminated in the fiery death of seventy-five Davidians, including more than a score of children in whose supposed interest the government had acted.

Once again, the ATF and FBI had forgotten the hard lessons that had been learned on that road outside Medina, North Dakota, in 1983, and then again, nine years later, at Ruby Ridge. Along with a lot of innocent people, they paid a steep price for that lapse of memory.

Once again, members of the Patriot movement voiced outrage. They saw Waco as further evidence of the government's increasing encroachment on the Bill of Rights and as confirmation of their most dire fears. Clive Doyle, who survived the blaze but lost a daughter to it, put it this way: "Waco is a wake-up call for people in the sense that they saw their government at work against citizens, perhaps for the first time."

Kirk Lyons saw the Waco case as "nothing more or

less than evidence of an ongoing pattern of federal abuse and murder.

"It's nothing more complicated than that. It's been going on for many years, but has not been noticed by the average citizen, because the number of casualties has generally been so minimal," he said. "I mean, when you polish off . . . Gordon Kahl or people like Robert Mathews, any of these so-called 'white separatist kooks'—which is the way they've been portrayed by the media—most Americans say 'good riddance.'

"Unfortunately, the average American does not recognize these incidents as evidence of a pattern of ongoing federal abuse."

The Patriot movement wasn't alone in decrying the carnage. Under a new, more radical leadership that vowed never to compromise on gun control legislation, the 3.5-million-member National Rifle Association used equally strident tones in condemning the government's actions. The group called Waco the opening salvo in the war to determine whether Nazi-like agents in the federal government would strip Americans of their God-given right under the Second Amendment to bear arms.

Still, it wasn't until later in 1993, when the Congress passed the Brady Bill, that the militia movement ignited into a nationwide brushfire. No longer were the voices raised in outrage only those belonging to members of the Patriot movement or the hard-line leadership of the NRA. Now the chorus included the voices of thousands of Americans who feared their guns would be forcibly taken, just as Randy Weaver and the Branch Davidians had had their weapons taken. Many would even join the militia ranks.

The blaze that erupted over the Brady Bill—a modest measure that imposed a five-day waiting period in the sale of all handguns and required background checks on potential gun buyers—intensified with the passage of the 1994 federal crime bill and its ban on the sale of certain semiautomatic weapons and its ten-bullet limit on gun clips.

The paramilitary right's weapon of choice had always been the assault rifle.

"A pistol won't be enough when a serious breakdown of order occurs," William Pierce noted in the November 1993 issue of the *National Alliance Bulletin*. "For serious killing an assault rifle is almost a necessity."

Beam had warned his racist militia group in the 1980s that one day serious killing weapons like assault rifles would be banned. Pierce, too, had predicted such legislation in *The Turner Diaries*.

> What a blow [the gun raid] was to us! And how it stunned us! All that brave talk by patriots, "The government will never take my guns away," and then nothing but meek submission when it happened.
>
> On the other hand, maybe we should be heartened by the fact that there were still so many of us who had guns then, nearly 18 months after the Cohen Act had outlawed all private ownership of firearms in the United States.

But it was not until the NRA mounted its scare campaign— after President Clinton moved to ban the sale of certain assault weapons—that the message began to sink in with Middle Americans already skeptical of government and frightened by crime.

"A document secretly delivered to me reveals frightening evidence that the full-scale war to crush your gun rights has not only begun, but is well underway," warned NRA Executive Vice President Wayne LaPierre in the group's June 1994 *American Rifleman* magazine.

"What's more," he continued, "dozens of federal gun bills suggest this final assault has begun—not just to ban all handguns or all semi-automatics, but to eliminate private firearms ownership completely and forever. I firmly believe the NRA has no alternative but to recognize this attack and counter with every resource we can muster."

The early calls to action were posted in gun stores and handed out at gun shows that brought together those who had tired of the paintball war games of the 1980s and others who just loved guns, where paramilitary fanatics like Timothy McVeigh and Terry Nichols sold weapons, racist propaganda, and militia manuals.

The Vietnam War produced hard-core militia leaders like Louis Beam. It also left millions angry at government and unsure of America's role in the world. Brave men fought, many felt, with one hand tied behind their backs by liberal politicians who supposedly refused to let our troops win. The enemy was on the banks of the Potomac River as well as in the Mekong Delta. Now the politicians, led by a "draft-dodging" president, wanted to strip weekend warriors of assault weapons. Other guns might be next.

James Gibson, doing research for his book, *Warrior Dreams: Paramilitary Culture in Post-Vietnam America*, attended the famous American Pistol Institute in Pauldin, Arizona, to master combat weapons. After a grueling week, he reflected on why the students, including a $25,000-a-year lumberjack, a $250,000-a-year doctor, a long-haired music student, and an elementary school teacher, each paid $600 to attend.

> In a world where most men have no real power or control over their lives, mastering a weapon is a kind of grand "compensation" price: *I'm not rich. I'm not*

> *politically powerful. The news media doesn't call me up*
> *and ask me what I think about things. I don't have*
> *scores of beautiful women after me. But, by God, I can*
> *kill anything that moves within 35 yards of me and*
> *have a good time doing it. I have that much power,*
> *anyway. I may never use it, but I know I've got the*
> *power if anyone ever tries to mess with me.*

"Buying a combat weapon," wrote Gibson, "is like joining a tribe; each weapon is a specific tribal totem. Men can belong to more than one tribe, however. The more weapons the warrior owns, the more power he can appropriate from their histories, and the more fantasy adventure he can pursue."

The NRA was not alone in getting out the word that gun lovers might soon lose whatever power and satisfaction owning a gun provided. Larry Pratt, executive director of Gun Owners of America, encouraged gun-loving citizens to form armed citizen militias as a way to get directly involved in the Second Amendment debate. He condemned the NRA as too quick to compromise. He appeared on dozens of radio talk shows repeating his message.

> [I]n times of national rebellion against the Lord
> God, the rulers of the nation will reflect the spiritual
> degradation of the people. The result is a denial of
> God's commandments, an arrogance of officialdom,
> *disarmament*, and oppression.

The message reaching the heartland was giving the new militia movement a powerful issue not dependent on racism. White men, and even an occasional black, flocked to join private armies from Michigan to Maine. The NRA gave the movement a backhanded blessing in a statement issued in November 1994, just a few months before Timothy McVeigh met with a unit of the Michigan Militia.

> Although the NRA has not been involved in the formation of any citizen militia units, neither has the NRA discouraged, nor would the NRA contemplate discouraging, exercise of a constitutional right.

When ATF agents made their final assault on Koresh's Waco compound, the climate for expanding the militias was white-hot. The NRA's electronic bulletin board contained a blunt message from its board member, Harry Thomas.

> And Miss Reno, I say to you: If you send your jack-booted, baby-burning bushwhackers to confiscate my guns, pack them a lunch—it will be a damn long day. The Branch Davidians were amateurs. I'm a professional.

In that intense climate, extremists such as William Pierce saw opportunity.

"The current campaign . . . to disarm Americans has many people angrier than anyone can imagine who is not in touch with what might be called 'the weapons culture,'" Pierce wrote in February 1994. "What this means is we have a great opportunity now to make an impression on a very receptive audience, if we move aggressively and use a reasonable degree of discretion.

"Gun shows provide a natural recruiting environment. Many more are being held now than ever before, and many more people are attending them."

No group was more aggressive than MOM—the Militia of Montana—in taking advantage of the opportunity Pierce saw.

# Militia
# Warriors

The Militia of Montana (MOM) was established in February 1994—a month before the Brady Bill went into effect—by John Trochmann, his brother David, and David's son Randy.

John Trochmann was at the police barricades at Ruby Ridge when lawmen went after his friend Randy Weaver. After the siege, Trochmann had joined with Identity adherent Chris Temple to form the United Citizens for Justice, a support group for Randy Weaver. Louis Beam was an early ally. Although the UCJ soon broke up due to internal bickering over strategy, it provided the foundation for the militias that both Trochmann and Stetson later established.

From the tiny town of Noxon, Montana, just fifty miles from Ruby Ridge, MOM quickly became one of the most prominent and influential of the militia groups. Its newsletter, *Taking Aim*, was widely read in militia circles. And its mail-order operation provided militia members with books, videotapes, and manuals on everything from how to form militias to how to prepare for war.

To the Trochmanns, the standoffs at Ruby Ridge and Waco and the passage of the Brady Bill all pointed to the same irrefutable conclusion: the proponents for the New World Order were making their move.

"There are individuals in this world, within this country, and in our own government who would like to rule the world. . . . These power hungry individuals have corrupted our government and are working on sabotaging our freedom by destroying the Constitution of the United States, in order to establish the 'New World Order,'" stated one MOM publication. "To bring about this New World Order, and ultimately the single World Government, . . . the American people must be disarmed."

Gun control means people control, said John Trochmann, whose full gray beard and stern eyes evoked a striking resemblance to an Old Testament patriarch. The Brady Bill marked the first step to acquiring that control. Ruby Ridge and Waco provided ample evidence of the government's willingness to wage war against its own citizens who refuse to relinquish their weapons and constitutional freedoms.

The only way for "ordinary Americans" to prevent any future "gun grabs" and atrocities such as Ruby Ridge and Waco, said Trochmann, was to come together under the banner of an unorganized militia.

"The security of a free state is not found in the citizens having guns in the closet," MOM argued in its militia manual. "It is found in the citizenry being trained, prepared, organized, equipped and [led] properly so that if the government uses its force against the citizens, the people can respond with a superior amount of arms, and appropriately defend their rights."

As important as gun control was to MOM's effort to build the militia movement, it wasn't MOM's only concern. It saw the government's attempt to strip Americans of their Second Amendment rights as just one in a long line of betrayals.

"When government allows our military to be ordered and controlled by [the United Nations], allows foreign armies to train on our soil, allows our military to label caring patriots as the enemy, then turns their tanks loose on U.S. citizens to murder and destroy, or directs a sniper to shoot a mother in the face while holding her infant in her arms, you bet [we're] upset," Trochmann told a U.S. Senate committee.

Americans have a right to be upset, he added, "when the average citizen must work for half of each year just to pay their taxes, while billions of our tax dollars are . . . sent to bail out the banking elite; while our fellow Americans are homeless, starving, and without jobs."

In its various publications and pamphlets, MOM pointed to laws regarding abortion, taxation, and home schooling as further examples of a government out to destroy an honored way of life. It maintained that the government—through affirmative action and set-aside programs—favored minorities, homosexuals, feminists, and a host of other groups over white Christian citizens. It contended that trade treaties, such as GATT and NAFTA, sent high-paying manufacturing jobs overseas and left white, Anglo-Saxon males with menial, low-paying work that does not allow them to support their families. It also contended that those treaties—engineered by the United Nations and the wealthy elite—represented the first step toward a one-world economy. MOM saw the government at the heart of a conspiracy to take guns away from true patriots, tax them into poverty, strip them of their constitutional rights, and place them under the boot of a one-world government.

To those who doubted the existence of the conspiracy, MOM handed out literature about sightings of black helicopters ferrying United Nations troops into positions for the eventual takeover of the United States; distributed maps showing how the New World Order plans to divide the United States into ten regions; displayed photographs of alleged concentration camps being built to intern anyone who might challenge the takeover; and told tales of 100,000 Hong Kong lawmen being brought into the country to police the takeover once it was complete.

Again, the last line of defense—the only line of defense—against such "tyranny, globalism, moral relativism, humanism, and the New World Order threatening to undermine these United States of America" was the unorganized militia.

In leading the militia drive, John Trochmann often portrayed himself, his supporters, and his allies as modern-day minutemen, the true heirs to the legacy of the American Revolution.

"To balance the military power of the nation with the might of the militia will put at odds any scheme by government officials to use the force of government against the people," MOM's militia handbook noted. "Therefore, when the codes and statutes are unjust for the majority of people, the people will rightly revolt and the government will have to acquiesce without a shot being fired, because the militia stands vigilant in carrying out the will of the people in defense of rights, liberty and freedom."

To be prepared to fight a Second American Revolution, MOM encouraged its members to arm themselves with, among other items, a combat knife, an AR-15 semiautomatic rifle, and six hundred rounds of .223 ammunition. It also encouraged members to study *The Art of War, Guerrilla Warfare and Special Forces Ops,*

*Sniper Training and Employment,* and *Unconventional Warfare Devices and Techniques.*

Those are just four of the titles included in MOM's sixteen-page mail-order catalog that contains fifty-one videotapes, forty-eight books and manuals, and eighteen audiotapes. Yet another item for sale is the *M.O.D. Training Manual,* a two-hundred-page, $75 book that outlines the biblical and ideological justification for a guerrilla war in the United States and provides details on how to conduct such an action. Among its directives are:

- Raiding armories in order to seize "arms, ammo and explosives."
- Coordinating sabotage attacks to cripple the economy of the country, agricultural or industrial production, transport and communications systems, the military, and police systems.
- Conducting a campaign of domestic terrorism that includes actions "usually involving the placement of a bomb or fire explosion of great destructive power, which is capable of effecting irreparable loss against the enemy."
- Executing spies, government officials, and anyone else who, of their own free will, go to the police to "supply clues and information and finger people" in paramilitary groups.

Still other titles a person can acquire through MOM's mail-order business include *The Road Back,* written by the late Posse Comitatus founder and Identity architect William Potter Gale; *Unfriendly Persuasion,* an anti–law enforcement book written by Identity author Maynard Campbell; and *Big Sister Is Watching You,* a book about "Hillary's hell cats, or if you like, Gore's Whores. [T]hese are the women who tell Bill Clinton what to do."

\*      \*      \*

Probably MOM's bestseller—and its greatest contribution to the movement—was its own manual that detailed how to form a militia. MOM mailed out thousands of those manuals to groups and individuals throughout the country.

Once the seeds were planted, it didn't take long for other militias to sprout. Among the first were the United States Militia Association of Idaho, the Unorganized Militia of Ohio, the Free Militia of Wisconsin, the Unorganized Militia of Stevens County (Washington), the Texas Light Infantry, the Florida State Militia, and the Michigan Militia Corps.

The Michigan Militia—destined to become the country's largest—was formed in April 1994 by Baptist minister and gun store owner Norman Olson and real estate agent Ray Southwell. Although John Trochmann has claimed partial responsibility for its formation, Olson granted most of the credit to Southwell.

Olson said Southwell came to him with the idea after he had lost a fight with the public school board over Goals 2000 and outcome-based education. Southwell saw the federally approved curriculum as a big-government, big-business ploy to weaken instruction, corrupt the educational system, and create little more than robots for the workplace.

"Ray came to me and said we needed to do something—we need to form a militia to defend our rights under the Constitution," said Olson.

But like MOM, the Michigan Militia was not a single-issue entity.

It wanted to get the federal government out of Michigan. "When you turn over state law to federal law, you also turn over the power to enforce that law," Olson said. "You give up your sovereignty and get more and more intrusion by the Environmental Protection

Agency, the Bureau of Forestry and other government agencies. We're gradually losing our state sovereignty."

And, naturally, the Michigan Militia was strongly opposed to gun control.

"[T]he Second Amendment is really the First in our country," Olson explained, "because without guns for protection from tyrants, we would have no free speech."

Soon after it was established, the Michigan Militia grew to between six thousand and seven thousand members, according to credible estimates.

One of those members was Mark Koernke, who would later break with the group and form his own group, the Michigan Militia at Large.

By day, Koernke was a janitor at a dormitory at the University of Michigan. But at night, he became "Mark from Michigan," a leading propagandist for the militia movement. Each night on his hour-long, nationwide shortwave radio program, "Intelligence Report," Koernke outlined the steps Americans had to take to defend themselves against the coming New World Order. According to Koernke, a secret national police force comprised of National Guardsmen, Los Angeles street gangs, and Nepalese Gurkhas will disarm the public; a division of Russian troops are bivouacked in salt mines beneath Detroit awaiting orders to rise and take over the United States; and before the United Nations takes control on behalf of the New World Order, the Federal Emergency Management Agency (FEMA) will establish an interim government.

It all sounded like bad science fiction.

But it was science fiction some people wanted to hear.

"I want to know more about what is going on. I think it's important that people try to learn as much as they can about what is going on in the country,"

Pennsylvania state representative Teresa Brown, who introduced Koernke at a February 1995 meeting in Meadville that attracted approximately one thousand people, told a reporter.

Much of Koernke's stump speech was taken from his self-produced videotape, *America in Peril,* which is widely screened by militia movement members.

At one point in his tape, Koernke addressed the camera holding a Russian-made Kalashnikov rifle and a roll of nylon rope.

"Now, I did some basic math the other day, not New World Order math, and I found that using the old-style math you can get about four politicians for about 120 foot of rope. And, by the way, Dupont made this. It is very fitting that one of the New World Order crowd should provide us with the resources to liberate our nation," he tells his audience. "Remember, whenever using it, always try and find a willow tree. The enter-tainment will last longer."

The smirk on Koernke's face as he urged his viewers to find a willow tree reminded me of the smiling faces of Klansmen in the old 1920s lynching photographs.

Not every individual militia unit established had racist ties. Some were formed by people who really believed the units provided a legitimate way to express their anger and frustration with a government that had grown too distant and, in some cases, hostile.

These militia members loved their country and believed in all that was outlined by the Constitution. They weren't haters, and they didn't want to associate with haters. They were working people, not goose-stepping Hitlerites. They monitored their group's membership closely. The neo-Nazis and skinheads were asked to leave. So were the bomb makers and bomb throwers.

But it was clear, by the summer of 1994, that the links between the movement as a whole and the haters and racists of America were strong.

Articles and advertisements that extolled the militias and endorsed Louis Beam's leaderless resistance strategy had appeared in racist and anti-Semitic publications such as the Identity-steeped *Jubilee*, the White Aryan Resistance's *WAR*, and the *Spotlight*, a slick weekly newspaper published by the Liberty Lobby. Telephone hot lines, computer bulletin boards, and the American Patriot Fax Network revealed ever more militia connections with the racist right.

Apart from MOM, Beam's leaderless resistance structure had been adopted by the Unorganized Militia of Idaho and the U.S. Taxpayers Party of Wisconsin, whose widely circulated *Free Militia* handbook strongly recommended the strategy. Other militias in Florida, Texas, Kansas, Missouri, Utah, and Colorado also adopted the structure or variations of it.

Militia groups also had embraced much of the dogma of the Posse Comitatus. Lawmen in Montana, Michigan, and elsewhere had reported an increasing number of militia members being stopped for driving without licenses or license plates. Such conduct is a form of severation, a central Posse Comitatus practice that encourages people to reclaim their sovereignty by returning—or simply tearing up—their driver's licenses, Social Security cards, and any other government-issued documents that intrude upon their God-given individual rights.

Militias in Montana, Michigan, and Idaho also were trying to enact into law the Posse tenet that all power rests at the county level and with the county sheriff. In each of those states, the militias sponsored legislation that would require federal authorities to notify the county sheriffs before any arrest could be made.

While John Trochmann had acknowledged past associations with racists such as Louis Beam and organizations such as the Aryan Nations, he insisted they were fleeting. He fervently denied that either he or his organization was racist.

"I don't have any animosities against Jewish people," he said.

At the same time, Trochmann noted at lectures and speaking engagements around the country that the people behind the one-world conspiracy were the "Anti-Christ banksters. The Warburgs and the Rothschilds. The Federal Reserve, and its chairman Alan Greenspan."

Trochmann's attempt to distance himself from any racist affiliation followed chapter and verse the script written at the Rocky Mountain Rendezvous. Downplay the racism, play up the antigovernment rhetoric. The fervor he displayed in separating himself from the white supremacists, however, prompted a sharp rebuke from one of the Estes Park participants.

Richard Butler, leader of the Aryan Nations, called Trochmann an anti-Christ for downplaying his association with that group. He said Trochmann had visited the Hayden Lake compound "quite often" and had attended at least six or seven Christian Identity Bible study meetings. Trochmann had even "helped us write out a set of rules for our code of conduct on church property," Butler said in his sharply worded press release.

Floyd Cochran, a former member of the Aryan Nations, was equally emphatic.

"John Trochmann can deny it all he wants but the fact is, he has had a long-standing relationship with the Aryan Nations and its followers," wrote Cochran in a letter to the *Ravalli* (Montana) *Republic.* "I know, because I was there.

"I had the opportunity to meet with the Trochmann family and deal with them both on a personal, and professional level, sharing with [them] the same beliefs of white supremacy and the role of government based on the racist faith of Christian Identity."

Cochran noted that Trochmann often "spoke at length on the merits of using the Bible and God, not the swastika and Hitler, to advance his brand of racism, bigotry, and Christian Identity."

From teaching skinheads the Christian Identity values at their home in the summer of 1990 to holding church services at the Aryan Nations compound, the "Trochmanns are respected leaders in the organized racist movement in Montana and Idaho," Cochran concluded.

Other leading racists who had found their way into the militia movement included James Wickstrom, the former self-proclaimed director of counterinsurgency for the Posse Comitatus. He operated an interstate communications network that targeted militias and white separatists out of an Identity church in Ulysses, Pennsylvania. As part of that network, Wickstrom, who had served prison time for impersonating a state official and for counterfeiting, had a 900 number hot line called "Fed-Up American" that spewed anti-Semitic conspiracy venom against "Jewish international bankers and their satanic New World Order" at $2 a minute. "Fed-Up American" also shared a post office box in Noxon, Montana—home of the Trochmanns and the Militia of Montana—with an Identity group called Yahweh's Covenant Mission.

In Texas, Bob Holloway, a Beam associate, organized the Texas Light Infantry. In Florida, Klansman Hank Pritchard left Robert Pummer's Florida State Militia and

established another unit north of Tampa with Jim
Palmer, the state's Aryan Nations director. In Colorado,
Duncan Philp, who was closely aligned with Pete Peters,
formed the White Patriots Militia in Fort Collins, and
Stewart Webb, a longtime anti-Semite, organized the
Guardians of American Liberties in Boulder.

Much like a tick buried in the thick hair on a dog's
neck, Beam, Peters, and the others had embedded
themselves into the militia movement and had helped
set its agenda.


It was not surprising that white supremacists were
preying upon the misfortune and anger of others to
enlarge their membership rolls. Nor was it surprising
that white supremacists were engaged in paramilitary
activities that ranged from rifle and pistol marksmanship to bomb making to hand-to-hand combat training.

Ever since Reconstruction and the evolution of the
Ku Klux Klan—under the direction of legendary
Confederate cavalry officer Gen. Nathan Bedford
Forrest—from a social club into a guerrilla-style, vigilante group, racists and haters have used paramilitary
units and militias both as a means of preserving white
supremacy and as a recruiting tool.

Following the 1954 U.S. Supreme Court ruling that
ordered the desegregation of the schools, the White
Citizens' Council and a reborn Ku Klux Klan sought to
exploit the fears many southerners had that they were
losing their white, American way of life. The two groups
attempted to thwart desegregation efforts and later
block the advances of the civil rights movement
through physical and economic intimidation of blacks
and their supporters.

Their terror, which included the bombings and

killings of those who stood before them, was no match for the moral force that animated the civil rights movement. While cowardly Klansmen could kill some people, thousands more were ready to take their place in picket lines throughout the South. By the mid-1960s, the civil rights movement—a movement that had its great leaders but was carried by the marching feet of ordinary men and women—was an irresistible force. With the passage of the Civil Rights Act of 1964 and the Voting Rights Act of 1965, the battle against the formal system of segregation was won. Unable to stem the tide and under attack from the FBI and congressional investigations, the Klan retreated, and its ranks dwindled.

In the late 1970s and early 1980s, the country saw a resurgence in Klan and neo-Nazi activity as economic times toughened. In secret locations across the country, white supremacists began arming themselves and training for what they believed and hoped would be the coming race war. They also tried, with limited success, to recruit among the growing number of fishermen, farmers, loggers, steelworkers, and others who through little, if any, fault of their own making were finding that hard work, a strong faith in God, and service to country and community were no longer guarantees to success.

In the mid-1980s, a racist youth movement from England—skinhead gangs—was imported to the United States. Although it emerged independently of organized white supremacist groups in this country, old-line Klan and neo-Nazi leaders rushed to embrace them. They enlisted skinheads as security guards, appeared with them on television talk shows, and solicited their participation in national gatherings such as the Aryan World Congress and the annual Stone Mountain Klan rally in Georgia. And the skinheads—young, reckless, and anxious to prove their courage as radical racists—quickly became the most violent of white supremacists. Since 1987, the skinheads have been responsible for more than thirty-five deaths and thousands of assaults against blacks, Asians, and gays.

But these street punks with their strange dress, pierced ears, avant music, and drug habits didn't fit the clean-cut, clean-living image promoted by Beam, Peters, Butler, and the other far-right leaders. The skinheads also proved to be an unstable lot. They picked dumb street fights that brought unwanted attention and could not be easily organized. Sometimes they even turned upon their elders. At a "White Man's Weekend" in Georgia, a group of skinheads beat Dennis Mahon, the leader of the Oklahoma branch of the White Aryan Resistance, within an inch of his life after he rubbed them the wrong way.

The racist movement had some very limited success in its prison ministries. The most widely known was established in 1979 by the late Michigan Identity minister and Klan leader Robert Miles, who served time in a federal penitentiary for burning school buses. White supremacist prisoners have proven records of violence and crime; their views are typically hardened by prison life; and they sometimes emerge from prison eager to spread the gospel of hatred and violence.

The Klan's greatest success in recent years had come when it gave its members an opportunity not just to burn crosses but to shoot bullets. It was no coincidence that Louis Beam's Texas Klan and Glenn Miller's Carolina Klan had been the most vibrant neo-Nazi groups of the 1980s. Both operated paramilitary wings that attracted new recruits and instilled a sense of discipline and purpose into the organizations' members. A nobody in the real world could be a captain in a Klan army.

With their explicit racist rhetoric and the baggage of

the Ku Klux Klan name, what the groups hadn't given the movement was the broad recruiting base or an entry into middle-class America it sought.

The new militia movement did that.

The movement, after all, was an ideal place for the white supremacists. It gave them almost everything they wanted: guns, paramilitary training, disenchantment and dissatisfaction with government, a recruiting pool much larger than any they'd ever had before, and public acceptance. It also was more politically correct to be a member of a militia—"a giant neighborhood watch," as Trochmann described it—than it was to be a card-carrying Klansman or Aryan Nations member.

As the militias' "neighborhood watch" began to expand, my colleagues and I at the Southern Poverty Law Center began watching them.

# Recipe for Disaster

At first, we looked at the new militia movement with curiosity.

We were concerned that white supremacists would get heavily involved because we felt that militias would attract those who were disgruntled and had a penchant for violence. But we had hoped that the movement itself would quickly fizzle and that the Louis Beams of the world would move on to the next fire.

By August 1994, it was becoming increasingly clear that our hopes were misplaced. Militias were multiplying, and the evidence of white supremacist involvement was mounting. Our curiosity turned to deep concern.

Danny Welch, a longtime friend and the director of the Southern Poverty Law Center's Klanwatch Project, sounded the alarm.

"Morris, we're picking up more and more scary news about ties between the militias and the white supremacist world," said Danny as he sat down in my office. "Hell, Morris, it could be one of the most dangerous developments we've ever seen."

Danny had my attention.

Danny, a former police officer and onetime chief of security at the Center, and I had been through some rough times together. Danny had made the midnight run to guard me after the FBI informed me that I was next on a neo-Nazi group's hit list. More than once, he had acted as a human shield when escorting me from a motel to a courthouse and back again after we'd received threats against me because of the lawsuits we'd filed against the Ku Klux Klan and neo-Nazi groups. And not once in the ten years we had been together did I ever see him flinch or display fear.

Nor did I know him to exaggerate. The forty-four-year-old former robbery-homicide detective worked with facts.

It was clear the facts that he and his staff had been gathering on the militia movement had unnerved him.

I set aside the brief I had been reading before Danny entered my office. "What's going on?" I asked him.

"It looks like a repeat of what we saw in Texas and North Carolina, only on a much larger scale," Danny said.

In Texas, in 1981, we had battled Louis Beam and his Texas Emergency Reserve. Three years later we tangled with Glenn Miller and the private army of his Carolina Knights of the Ku Klux Klan.

An ex–Green Beret and former member of the National Socialist Party of America, Miller fashioned his Klan group into a paramilitary army that had more than a thousand members—many of them ex–military personnel—in the Carolinas and Virginia. The group terrorized minorities in the region.

One of their targets was Bobby Person, a black

prison guard from Monroe County, North Carolina, who sought to take a promotion exam just like the white officers. If he passed, Person would become the first black sergeant ever in the county prison system. To discourage him from going forward with the exam, Miller's militia followers burned a cross on the front lawn of his rural home, scratched the letters "KKK" into the hood of his father's pickup, harassed his wife and children while he was at work, and threatened to kill him.

When I spoke to Person about suing the Klan, I warned him the harassment could get much worse. He was unfazed. He would not back down.

After we filed a lawsuit in 1984, it was Miller who lost his will to fight. He accepted a court-sanctioned settlement in which he agreed to stop harassing blacks and to cease all paramilitary operations.

It was an agreement Miller didn't keep.

Some two years later, Klanwatch investigators discovered that Miller was rebuilding his army under the banner of the White Patriot Party, a group he described as a "citizens' militia" that had as its goal the creation of a "White Republic within the geographical bounds of the Southern United States."

We also uncovered evidence that Miller had purchased thousands of dollars of stolen military hardware and was using active-duty military personnel to train his citizens' militia in the use of antitank weapons, plastic explosives, and Claymore mines, and in the military arts of escape and evasion as well as hand-to-hand combat. In an effort to separate the neo-Nazi foot soldiers from their professional trainers, we disclosed the military link to Miller's men in a letter to Secretary of Defense Caspar Weinberger. It resulted in the issuance of an order that banned military personnel from participating in white supremacist groups.

We then filed a motion against Miller, his second in command Stephen Miller (no relation), and the White Patriot Party asking the court to hold them in criminal contempt for violating the order forbidding paramilitary operations. Following a one-week trial during which Center Legal Director Richard Cohen and I served as special prosecutors appointed by the court, a federal jury convicted the Millers. Both were sentenced to brief prison terms, but Stephen Miller's sentence was suspended and Glenn Miller was released on bond pending appeal.

We hadn't heard the last of the Millers.

Four White Patriot Party members were arrested just as they were about to rob a Fayetteville, North Carolina, restaurant. The men intended to use the money from the robbery organized by Stephen Miller to buy stolen military rockets and use them to blow up the Center and kill me. Soon after that plot failed, Glenn Miller broke his bond conditions, issued a "declaration of war" against the government, Jews, and blacks, and called for my assassination.

Miller mailed me a copy of his declaration, a rambling two-page document that began:

> *Dear White Patriots:*
> I warned the S.O.B.s . . . the federal dogs, to leave me alone. All 5,000 White Patriots are now honor bound and duty bound to pick up the sword and do battle against the forces of evil. Swear you'll not put down your sword until total victory is ours. Yahweh will fill your hearts with courage and strength and confidence. . . . Let the blood of our enemies flood the streets, rivers, and fields of the nation, in Holy vengeance and justice. . . . The Jews are our main and most formidable enemies. . . . They are truly the

children of Satan. Throw off the chains which bind
us to the satanic, Jewish controlled and ruled federal
government. The following point system for Aryan
warriors of The Order [for each kill]: Niggers (1),
White race traitors (10), Jews (10), Judges (50),
Morris Seligman Dees (888). Let the battle axes
swing smoothly and the bullets whiz true.

He signed his directive, "Glenn Miller, loyal member
of 'The Order.'" In court depositions, Miller had denied
being a member of Robert Mathews's outlaw group. But
in this burst of patriot courage, he came clean.

Miller was humiliated that ZOG agents had used a
simple contempt of court motion to gut his Aryan army.
He saw his death as imminent and requested burial "in
the Miller graveyard near Dillon, South Carolina, in my
White Patriot Party uniform." We took the threat seriously from this wounded white warrior.

The FBI tracked Miller and three of his aides, who
had gone underground in a van filled with weapons, to
a mobile home park near Springfield, Missouri. Just ten
short days after calling for mass murder and revolution,
Miller was forced from his hideout—a rented trailer—
half naked, his eyes burning from tear gas.

Partly because of our successes against the likes of
Beam and Miller, partly because of a vigorous campaign by the U.S. Justice Department to clamp down on
The Order, the Covenant, Sword and Arm of the Lord,
the Posse Comitatus, and other hate groups, and partly
because of infighting among the disparate groups, the
white supremacist movement was in disarray at the
beginning of the 1990s. In many respects, it was start-
ing to crumble, cave in on itself. No one at the Center's
Klanwatch Project lost any sleep over the movement's
misfortune.

But the flame of hatred was never extinguished.

I had seen the Klan's resurgence in the late 1970s and the rise of racist militia groups in the 1980s, but they did not find a major following, even in the Old South.

But now, a fanatic in Michigan was talking about lynchings on the airwaves and race baiters like Louis Beam were repackaging their hate messages to cheering crowds of Middle America malcontents.

It was clear we couldn't ignore the militia movement. As Julian Bond, a professor at the University of Virginia and president emeritus of the Southern Poverty Law Center, once noted, "History won't let me ignore current events. I turn on my television set and see people in Klan robes or military uniforms again handing out hate literature on the town square; I read in my newspaper of crosses again burned in folks' yards, and it seems as if we were back in the '60s.

"Those who would use violence to deny others their rights can't be ignored. The law must be exercised to stay strong. And even racists can learn to respect the law."

When we formed Klanwatch in 1979, we were accused of doing the Klan and neo-Nazi hate groups a favor. Critics said that reporting on the activities of hate groups and suing them in court would only give them valuable publicity.

But most of our critics became supporters as we defeated one hate group after another. These victories included a $7 million judgment against the once-power-ful United Klans of America for the lynching death of a black college student in Mobile, Alabama. It was the first time a Klan group had gone to trial for the acts of its members. The suit bankrupted the Klan group that had been responsible during the height of the civil rights struggle in the 1960s for beating the Freedom Riders, killing four young black girls by bombing the 16th Street Baptist Church in Birmingham, and murdering an activist during the historic Selma-to-Montgomery march for voting rights.

In 1987, the year after we shut down Miller's neo-Nazi army in North Carolina, we filed suit against the Klan groups that had led an assault against peaceful civil rights marchers in Forsyth County, Georgia. The case forced the Invisible Empire—then the country's largest Klan group—to fold.

Two years later, we filed suit against Tom Metzger and his neo-Nazi White Aryan Resistance after three members of the East Side White Pride, a Portland, Oregon, skinhead group, beat an Ethiopian immigrant to death with a baseball bat. We contended that the murder was a direct result of the training and direction that an agent for Metzger had given the Portland skinheads with Metzger's full approval. In 1990, a Portland jury agreed and assessed damages of $12.5 million, the largest in Oregon history, against Metzger, his son, and their WAR organization. Following the verdict, Metzger lost his house, and his hate business was crippled.

Something had to be done to counter the militias. We couldn't just wait for something bad to happen. We had to play militia catch-up. We had to find out where this expanding movement was heading and whether white supremacists were as deeply embedded in it as we feared. To accomplish these goals, we established a Militia Task Force within our Klanwatch Project to monitor the formation and infiltration of militias by white supremacists who hoped to exploit the movement's recruiting potential and its fierce antigovernment fervor.

Beginning in late August 1994, the task force began

collecting in a systematic fashion the growing reams of unsettling evidence that clearly indicated the direction of the militia movement.

This evidence weighed heavily on my mind when I took my annual motorcycle trip into the coal-mining country deep in the Appalachian Mountains to visit friends. My first time there was in 1976 when I took a break from Jimmy Carter's presidential campaign and rode from Alabama to Blackey, Kentucky. It was the place where the movie *Coal Miner's Daughter* was filmed. It also was the home of Joe Begley, a half-Cherokee, half-Scottish storekeeper I met through an idealist Methodist minister who once had a small church at the head of a deep hollow nearby.

Like much of Appalachia, Blackey is poor. A good number of its nine hundred residents are unemployed miners on food stamps, single mothers who appear middle-aged by the time they are thirty, and hourly coal haulers. Many look to Joe Begley for leadership in their fight to force absentee mine owners to be responsible corporate citizens.

As we sat on the double porch swing, next to the big buckeye tree shading his store, Joe asked me what the Center had been involved in lately. Joe sent us $10 now and then, and he kept our literature posted on the wall behind the cash register. He was proud to speak up for civil rights, and he often expressed sorrow at never having had the opportunity to march with Dr. Martin Luther King.

I told Joe about the militia movement and how it was gaining ground with people who didn't trust the government. I told him that my old enemy Louis Beam and his racist friends were working behind the scenes.

Although Joe would probably find a lot in common with those attracted to the militia movement, he saw good guys and bad guys clearly and was willing to fight anyone who stood in the way of America having a government that was for all the people.

"You ought to sue them," he said simply.

"Joe, you know I'd sue in a New York minute, just like we did the Klan bunch who lynched that man in Mobile," I replied. "But they haven't done anything we can nail them for yet."

As my excuse for not acting against the militia settled on Joe, I thought to myself: I know what these guys are up to and what they intend. Why wait? Maybe we don't have a client or a fire, but we do have suspects and a lot of smoke.

It was Saturday morning, October 1, 1994. I called Danny at his home from Joe's store and asked him to update the facts on the militia we had discussed in August and to try to have a report ready for me when I returned.

Danny didn't let me down.

"Identity followers are the single most dangerous element in the current militia movement," he wrote. "It's a movement fueled by religious fanaticism and racism, fully armed and willing to kill. Its members are capable of becoming Americanized versions of the kind of extremists you read about in other countries, a full-scale terrorist underground.

"For them, this is a holy war. One they intend to fight to the finish."

Danny concluded his report by stating: "The popularity of the militias, along with their conspiracy theories, rabid antigovernment rhetoric, and a willingness to take up arms, makes the movement highly attractive to longtime racist leaders. It gives them and their cohorts a public platform for their racist agenda and fertile ground for new recruits. It is a very volatile situation."

I agreed.

How serious did I take the threat? Did I believe those involved in the militia movement could fulfill their promised Second American Revolution?

Not hardly. I couldn't imagine the new militia movement—with its anti-Semitic, white supremacist, and Christian Identity underpinnings—gaining enough power and support to seriously challenge our democratic institutions.

Did I think they could hurt a lot of people along the way, even if they had no real hope of ultimate success?

Definitely.

Only fate had prevented Glenn Miller and his ragtag private army from exploding stolen military C-4 plastic explosives under a school bus filled with black children or under a hydroelectric power dam. In 1993, the police had uncovered thirteen explosives stockpiles and numerous bombing plots connected to the white supremacy movement. Only luck had prevented major catastrophes.

With the fire at Waco, the passion for vengeance against the federal government had intensified. Ruby Ridge was the militia's battle cry.

Who could say whether a relentless string of terrorist attacks on communications complexes, federal buildings, transportation systems, and public facilities would force our government to drastically increase police surveillance, angering many more into joining the extremists.

I knew this was the game plan of the far-right, racist-inspired paramilitary groups.

We couldn't sit on our information any longer.

On October 24, 1994, I went in my office, slipped a piece of paper into my old, manual Smith Corona, and started to type:

*Dear Attorney General Reno:*

On behalf of the Southern Poverty Law Center and its supporters, I urge you to alert all federal law enforcement authorities to the growing danger posed by the unauthorized militias that have recently sprung up in at least eighteen states. Some sources put this number as high as thirty.

We have substantial evidence that white supremacists are infiltrating the leadership of these organizations. In our view, this mixture of armed groups and those who hate is a recipe for disaster.

The Justice Department's own experience demonstrates that the danger is very real. In 1984, for example, federal prosecutors in Seattle obtained convictions of 22 members of The Order, an armed and fanatical white racist group bent on inciting a race war that would lead to the overthrow of the government. Those convicted had robbed armored cars of more than $4.1 million, stored caches of military weapons, killed a well-known person from Denver, and planned the murders of many other prominent citizens.

In 1986, the Justice Department helped stop the paramilitary operations of the North Carolina White Patriot Party after our office provided evidence that active-duty military personnel were assisting the group and providing military armament. White Patriot Party members were linked to many crimes, including three murders.

Our office has confirmed the active involvement of a number of well-known white supremacists, Posse Comitatus, Identity Christian, and other extremist leaders and groups in the growing militia movement. Those individuals involved include Louis Beam, once on the FBI's Ten Most Wanted list and now an Aryan Nations leader, James Wickstrom, a Posse Comitatus leader convicted of conspiracy to pass counterfeit bills to fund a guerrilla army, and James "Bo" Gritz, . . . who has been closely associated with David Duke and other white racist leaders.

We have also received reports that active-duty military personnel as well as National Guardsmen may be assisting some of the newly-formed militias. Based on our North Carolina experience, these reports are ominous.

Citizens have the right to form peaceful groups to protest gun legislation and to engage in target practice. But they do not have the right to possess illegal weapons, violate state paramilitary laws, or harass minorities. Based on the history of paramilitary operations conducted under the influence of white supremacists, I believe it is highly likely that illegal activity of this sort is already occurring.

I have enclosed a brief biographical sketch of some white supremacist leaders and others who are involved in the militia movement, a list of the militia groups receiving their help, and a list of state militia groups that have no known white supremacy involvement at this time.

Please feel free to contact me or my staff if we can be of assistance.

*Sincerely,*
*Morris Dees*

As I left for home the evening that I wrote this letter, I drove past the Civil Rights Memorial that graces the plaza in front of the Southern Poverty Law Center. Designed by Maya Lin, the artist who also designed the

Vietnam War Memorial, the Civil Rights Memorial honors those who died during the struggle for equality in this country and highlights key events from the era between 1954 and 1968. Inscribed on the curved black granite wall at the back edge of the memorial plaza is a line Dr. King borrowed from the Old Testament prophet Amos for his 1963 "I Have a Dream" speech. It reads:

### Until Justice Rolls Down Like Waters and Righteousness Like a Mighty Stream

A thin sheet of water flows down the face of the wall over these powerful words.

In the center of the plaza is a circular black granite table. Water that emerges from the center of the table flows evenly across it. Inscribed beneath the flowing water in lines that radiate from the table's center are the names of the martyrs of the civil rights movement. Between the first and last entry, Maya left a space to symbolize the martyrs who had been forgotten and those who would surely be killed in the future by the forces of intolerance.

As I drove, I hoped that what I had described as a "recipe for disaster" in my letter to Attorney General Reno would not add more names to a memorial that already reflected so much suffering.

# Winds of
# Rage

In the days before the November 1994 congressional elections, it was hard to find an audience that would appreciate the words of Martin Luther King, much less a warning about a possible disaster some unspecified time in the future.

Although my letter to the attorney general generated some public interest, it was impossible to turn the country's attention away from the "Contract with America" and the impending Republican sweep of Congress.

To me, the anti-Washington fervor was particularly ironic because it seemed to represent the triumph of the politics of my fellow Alabamian, George Wallace, a generation after his day. Wallace was, in the words of biographer Dan Carter, "the most influential loser in twentieth-century American politics." Commenting on Wallace's retirement from politics in 1986, the *New York Times*, striving to give him a proper place in history without rendering an endorsement, wrote that he had "sniffed out early the changes America came to know by many names: white backlash . . . the silent majority . . . the alienated voters . . . the emerging Republican majority."

It started on January 14, 1963, with a message that later proved to have as much appeal outside the Deep South as it did to thousands who braved the coldest day in eighty years to hear Wallace sworn in as governor of Alabama. I had supported him in his earlier, unsuccessful campaign for the office when he was endorsed by Alabama's progressive community and opposed by a popular Klan-backed attorney general. We parted company politically when Wallace vowed that he would "never be out-niggered again." Former Klansman Louis Beam could have drafted Wallace's inaugural address as well as Asa Carter, the Klansman to whom Wallace turned for the words that became the battle cry for die-hard segregationists throughout the South.

> Today I stand where once Jefferson Davis stood, and took an oath to my people. It is very appropriate then that from this Cradle of the Confederacy, this Heart of the Great Anglo-Saxon Southland . . . we sound the drum of freedom. . . . In the name of the greatest people that have ever trod this earth, I draw in the dust and toss the gauntlet before the feet of tyranny . . . and I say . . . segregation now . . . segregation tomorrow . . . and segregation forever.

After symbolically standing in the schoolhouse door to block integration at my alma mater, the University of Alabama, in 1963 and then promptly backing down to the federal government, Wallace was cheered outside the South by many angry whites who viewed court-ordered integration and busing as a threat to their neighborhood schools. Wallace blasted the Justice Department, federal officials, and federal judges on national news shows. Letters of support, many encouraging him to run for president, poured in by the thousands as he urged that control of public schools be returned to local government and be taken away from "bearded Washington bureaucrats who can't even park a bicycle straight."

In his campaign for the presidency, Wallace mined a new vein of white middle-class discontent in passionate speeches from Jackson, Mississippi, to New York's Madison Square Garden before packed audiences. Dan Carter observed in his book, *The Politics of Rage:*

> In speech after speech, Wallace knit together the strands of racism with those of a deeply rooted xenophobic "plain folk" cultural outlook which equated social change with moral corruption. The creators of public policy—the elite—were out of touch with hardworking taxpayers who footed the bills for their visionary social engineering at home and weakminded defense of American interest abroad.

Wallace recognized that his "segregation forever" image limited broad-based acceptance among conservative voters outside the South. In 1972, I was George McGovern's national finance director when Wallace was making his third try for the White House. He was saying one thing outside Alabama and another here at home. Like racist militia leaders Louis Beam and Pete Peters, he had a public and private message.

Bullets cut short Wallace's full participation in the conservative groundswell that elected Richard Nixon, Ronald Reagan, and George Bush and paved the way for Republican control of Congress in 1994, but he anticipated the issues and voiced the concern. Newt Gingrich rode into power demanding decentralized government, but it was Wallace who said on *Meet the Press* in 1968 that he would pull out of the race if the remaining candidates would pledge "to turn back local institutions to the state." He was polling 20 percent as a third-party candidate and threatening to throw the election into the House of Representatives for the first time since 1825. He drew thunderous cheers and millions in $10 to $25 gifts, damning welfare cheats, urban rioters, "bleeding-heart liberals," and especially "out-of-touch politicians." Wallace condemned politics as usual, finding not "ten cents worth of difference" between the two major parties.

His effect on the national debate remains. "[H]is attacks on the federal government have become the gospel of modern conservatism; his angry rhetoric the foundation for the new ground rules of political warfare," Dan Carter observed.

This political warfare found new generals. Richard Nixon defeated Wallace with his "Southern Strategy," convincing white voters he could deal more effectively with welfare cheats, minority-caused crime, and liberal Democrats. Ronald Reagan seized divisive issues like abortion and gun control and launched a conservative political revolution aimed at demolishing New Deal programs and severely reducing the role of the federal government. Jimmy Carter refused to buy into racism and government bashing. His campaign and administration were an oasis in a political desert.

Candidates like Jesse Helms and George Bush crossed back over the line Wallace abandoned by resorting to overt racism. Helms won a narrow bid for North Carolina's U.S. Senate seat in 1990 over black Charlotte mayor Harvey Gantt using a television commercial exploiting white anger over affirmative action. The spot showed a white man's hands holding a "job rejection" letter. As the hands crumpled the letter, a voice-over said:

You need that job. And you were the best quali-
fied. But they gave it to a minority because of a racial
quota. Is that really fair?

Then, as the screen pictures Helms's black opponent, the voice continues, "Gantt supports . . . racial
quota laws that make the color of your skin more
important than your qualifications."

President Bush, playing on the fears of whites, ran
the now infamous Willie Horton television spot, pictur-
ing a black inmate on work release who had sexually
assaulted a white woman. The woman was shown in
her white wedding dress, the black in handcuffs,
disheveled and unkempt.

The 1992 presidential campaign brought more blatant and strident appeals to white America's fears of
minorities and distrust of government. Candidates Ross
Perot and Pat Buchanan mobilized a highly vocal
minority with attacks on immigration, welfare cheats,
trade treaties, crime, and federal government regulations. These losing campaigns left their followers seeking new ways to vent their frustrations.

Newt Gingrich provided them and millions of other
Americans fed up with politics as usual an outlet for
their anger—the Contract with America. This ten-point
document covered all the bases: effective death penalty
provisions, prohibiting funds to minor mothers, cuts in
social spending, funds for prison construction, term lim-
itations to replace career politicians with citizen legislators, and a balanced budget/tax limitation amendment.
These pledges, and others in the Contract, were seen by
angry citizens as efforts to take control of government
from criminal-prone, welfare-supported minorities and
their liberal representatives.

The warfare George Wallace unleashed was not only

picked up on by politicians, but it spread like a brush-fire across a dry Alabama sage patch, jumping from the political arena to the pulpits of fundamentalist preachers and into the appeals of single-issue conservative groups. But nowhere does the old Wallace message echo more loudly than on talk radio.

No talk show host has more consistently and effectively delivered antigovernment messages to the militia-infested heartland over the past four years than smooth, affable, 325-pound Chuck Harder. He is the king of grassroots airwaves.

"We have a government, ladies and gentlemen, that is lying to the people, raping the people, defrauding the people," Chuck Harder said during his three-hour radio call-in show carried on over three hundred mainly small-town stations in forty-six states. "These [federal officials] are very power hungry and, in my opinion, evil people. They want all the marbles."

Had Timothy McVeigh tuned to KBYR while visiting his army buddy Michael Fortier in Kingman, Arizona, he might have heard a similar message from Harder from 2:00 to 5:00 P.M. or during two daily replays. While traveling from Kansas to Oklahoma City in his rented Ryder truck, he could have heard Harder on eight different stations advertise videotapes about government-implanted computer chips designed to enslave American citizens. And, while locked in the Perry, Oklahoma, jail, McVeigh might have heard Harder's broadcast from KSIW in nearby Woodward suggesting that President Clinton resorted to homicide as a cover-up: "The difference between Watergate and Whitewater is a very, very big pile of bodies."

His Peoples Radio Network, broadcasting from the

historic Telford Hotel on the banks of the Suwannee River in White Springs, Florida, features a twenty-four-hour-a-day, seven-day-a-week lineup, including news on the hour. Seven months before the Oklahoma City bombing, Harder added a thirty-minute television talk show now carried on eighty stations.

His style and voice are a blend of Mike Wallace and Peter Jennings, credible, authoritative, nonconfrontational; he's a self-anointed spokesman for George Wallace's forgotten and angry "little people." Dion Cole, a Florida highway patrolman, told CNN, "I believe what he says because he's done his research, and surely he couldn't say it over the radio if it wasn't fact."

Chuck Harder's audience is so loyal that more than forty thousand pay at least $15 a year to belong to his nonprofit "For the People" organization. Another thirty thousand pay an extra $19 a year to subscribe to his biweekly thirty-two-page *News Report*. Uplink satellite dishes dot the lawn of the once-abandoned hotel he bought and renovated to produce his shows and house his sixty-two employees. For the People took in more than $4 million in 1994 alone, all nontaxable, in membership fees and mail-order merchandise sales. Backed by his army of loyal subscribers, Harder can offer programming free to grateful low-budget stations.

Harder and other conservative talk radio hosts did not create the anger they tap. The frustration they voice—the same frustration that is fueling the Religious Right, neo-Nazi groups, and various other ultra-conservative movements—is complex and deeply rooted.

No dividing line neatly separates this century's domestic extremists. George Wallace ushered in a new mode of conservative politics in the late 1960s, but the distrust of government elites engendered by Joseph McCarthy in the 1950s accounted for some of the underlying feelings Wallace so skillfully manipulated.

The messages and the messengers reaching the heartland from television pulpits, political commercials, and talk radio mikes have inbred family trees. A year before the Oklahoma City disaster, Reverend Pat Robertson took aim at the government on his *700 Club* with a message Louis Beam, Pete Peters, or William Pierce would have been proud to deliver.

> I do believe this year that there's going to be persecutions against Christians. The government frankly is our enemy and we're going to see more and more of the people who have been placed in office last year . . . getting control of the levers of power and they will begin to know how to use them and they'll use them to hurt those who are perceived as their enemies.

Pat Robertson's Christian Coalition borrowed from Jerry Falwell's earlier Moral Majority. The prayer cloths of both contain threads from prior right-leaning leaders like Barry Goldwater as well as more from recent ones like Phyllis Schlafly of Eagle Forum and Paul Weyrich of the Free Congress Foundation.

Economic uncertainty, job insecurity, corporate downsizing, declining real wages, changing technology, and competition from cheap foreign labor are scaring people to death. Corporations report higher earnings, executives earn huge salaries, stock markets hit new highs, but the average worker feels abandoned and betrayed. The nation that was so confident after coming home victorious from World War II is now sure of nothing. We are, many feel, a nation in decline.

"The American dream of the middle class has all but disappeared, substituted with people struggling just to buy next week's groceries," wrote Timothy McVeigh in a letter published in his hometown newspaper, the

Lockport, New York, *Union-Sun Journal* in February 1992. "What is it going to take to open the eyes of our elected officials?"

That is a sentiment Harder has repeatedly expressed to his radio audience. "America is dying," Harder warned.

Angry, frustrated Americans want simple, not complicated answers. Many older Americans in rural areas remember gathering around the woodstove at the crossroads country store, sharing gripes with kindred neighbors and feeling a sense of community. Now they gather around the radio. The Chuck Harders shape the debate, targeting scapegoats, real or imagined.

Most urban Americans never hear Chuck Harder unless they pass through small towns like Hancock in Michigan, Chanute in Kansas, Roanoke in Alabama, Eden in North Carolina, or Bogalusa in Louisiana, and tune in as he "saves the little guy" from a wicked federal government in league with greedy corporations. Just nine days before the Oklahoma City bomb exploded, a commentator for *The Nation* put it this way:

> Harder's daily nostrums ricochet off the shuttered factories of the heartland and into the jarred consciousness of a mostly rural audience already scared out of its wits by the uncertainties of a rapidly changing America. Unlike Rush Limbaugh's straightforward propaganda for the Republican Party, Harder rallies his fervently loyal audience around a paranoid, conspiratorial vision, seasoned by facile scapegoating that in its worst moments degenerates into a vehicle for thinly veiled xenophobia and anti-Semitism. In sum, Harder isn't an antidote to Limbaugh; he is his country cousin.

Today, more than 1,000 commercial radio stations have all-talk formats, most covering news and issues. The vast majority of the hosts are conservative. Harder's

300 stations are second only to Limbaugh's 639. Other popular conservative and far-right hosts include G. Gordon Liddy with 225 stations and Pat Buchanan with 140. They overlap Harder's small-town audience and extend into major media markets. Popular conservative talk radio hosts from Limbaugh to Oliver North to Atlanta's Neal Boortz to Ken Hamblin, "the black avenger," to New York City's Bob Grant replay Harder's message to millions.

Many shortwave stations also carry antigovernment programs. Rick Tyler, broadcasting from WWCR 5.065 in Nashville, Tennessee, told his listeners that he "could talk for hours about the criminal conduct of our government. They are ruthless, they are cunning, they are cutthroat and, furthermore, we are their target."

"We are engaged in the most desperate war we have ever fought," William Pierce said from his Hillsboro, West Virginia, studio, "a war for the survival of our [white] race. Ultimately we cannot win it except by killing our enemies." He assured his solitary listeners bent over shortwave radios across the land that they were not alone in this holy struggle: "There are a hundred thousand or so of us here today listening to this program who aren't confused or ashamed or guilty."

Layer upon layer of irresponsible, inflammatory antigovernment rhetoric beamed daily from talk radio into the heartland feeds the militia agenda and, in some cases, provides direct support. Chuck Harder interviewed Ken Adams, a top officer of the Michigan Militia, for over an hour portraying his assault-trained, gun-toting private army as a friendly neighborhood watch group.

HARDER: So this is essentially citizens willing to be there in the time of need, maybe the way the American Radio Relay League is there for ham radio operators.
ADAMS: Absolutely.

HARDER: But you also want to be sovereign and not tied to the government; you don't want to be able to be called by . . . Janet Reno to go invade Waco?

ADAMS: Absolutely. We can't paint scenarios of what's liable to happen tomorrow. . . . If another Waco took place . . . the militias would be there by the thousands.

"The problem we have right now is who do we shoot?" a caller asked on Chuck Baker's Colorado Springs KVOK radio show in late 1994. "We're going to have to make plans. . . . You've got to get ammo. . . . We have to do it as an orchestrated militia."

Baker, a popular radio personality, seemed to endorse the caller's proposal. "Am I advocating the overthrow of this government? . . . I'm advocating the cleansing," he concluded while mimicking the sound of a firing pin. "K-ching, k-ching."

G. Gordon Liddy admitted using drawings of President and Mrs. Clinton for target practice and suggested shooting ATF agents in the head. He defended his words as harmless. "I don't believe I'm fueling the lunatic fringe," he said.

It may be hard to prove him incorrect, but the hatred and distrust for government fostered by talk radio and single-issue groups like Gun Owners of America and the National Rifle Association helped fuel the anger of citizens throughout the country and swell the militia ranks.

Gun control was not the issue on Dick Carver's mind as he climbed aboard his twenty-two-ton Caterpillar bulldozer on July 4, 1994. He drove directly toward an armed U.S. Forest Service agent who held a hand-lettered sign ordering him to stop. Two hundred neighbors, many armed, cheered Carver as he attempted to open a weather-damaged road across a national forest without first obtaining a federal permit. The agent backed down, making Carver a national hero in the Wise Use and county supremacy movement.

Wise Use is a loose network of right-wing grassroots groups and business interests that seeks to open federal land to virtually unlimited logging, mining, off-road vehicles, real estate development, and grazing. The fast-growing grassroots movement got its real start in the last days of the 1992 presidential campaign in reaction to Bill Clinton and Al Gore's highly touted environmental views.

A month after Carver's face-off with what he saw as "federal tyranny," a bomb demolished the van of a federal forest ranger in Carson City, Nevada. Then a bomb damaged a Carson City forest ranger office. No one has been arrested.

"[E]veryone here," a Nye County, Nevada, real estate agent told *Newsweek*, "would like to see a revolution and have the federal government washed away. But nobody wants a shooting war. We'd be annihilated."

Nye, like so many western counties, is vast, sparsely populated, and fiercely independent. It covers eighteen thousand square miles, an area nearly the size of Vermont and New Hampshire. It has barely more than one person per square mile. The federal government owns over 90 percent of the land. The local residents are fighting mad at the absentee landlord.

"I've told the Forest Service and the Bureau of Land Management, 'Don't be coming to me to render assistance if you take these people's property without due process,'" recalled Nye County sheriff Wade Lieseke Jr. "A forest ranger can take your cattle just by signing a piece of paper? A *forest ranger?* Give me a break."

I can understand this defiant, independent attitude. When meat was rationed during World War II, farmers were not allowed to kill cattle and distribute the beef. My father and I violated this rule, slaughtering cattle deep in the woods away from prying federal eyes. We gave the meat free to hungry people in our community.

I was angered when Department of Agriculture agents forced my father to plow up two acres of waist-tall cotton because he had mistakenly overplanted his government allotment. We had a small farm and times were hard. That destroyed cotton would have purchased needed shoes and school clothes for my sisters and brothers. I plowed under the lush stalks as the federal cotton-checker watched. I cursed him under my breath. How could someone tell us how to use our land?

As I look back now, I realize that the cotton acreage allotment program was approved by farmers as a way to reduce production and support prices. I have always doubted the wisdom of not allowing the free markets to weed out inefficient farmers and determine prices. But my father, like the western ranchers grazing leased federally owned land, was receiving a benefit for participating in the program. He knew the rules going in. Even so, people who live off the land feel they feed and clothe the nation, that they are owed. As a lawyer today, over fifty years since I stood lookout on the edge of the woods while my father shot the fattened steer, I still bridle at someone imposing one-size-fits-all rules.

Dick Carver's defiance of federal authority has been repeated numerous times across the West, often with militia support. He has spoken in twenty-three states to packed audiences.

By late 1994, more than thirty-five counties in Arizona, New Mexico, Nevada, and California had claimed sovereignty over federal lands inside their bor-

ders. Utah's representative Jim Hansen joined local officials like Sheriff Lieseke in wanting to remove federal
influence. Hansen derailed a plan to designate 5.7 million acres of Utah as wilderness and is seeking to open
an area near Bryce Canyon National Park to coal mining. Radio talk shows across the West spend hours condemning elitist environmentalists who, in the words of
Representative Don Young of Alaska, are a "waffle-
stomping, Harvard-graduating, intellectual bunch of
idiots."

In the weeks before the 1994 election, the Republicans,
sensing a sweep of both houses, removed all the stops.
They faxed talking points to 350 talk show hosts daily.
Democratic faxes went to fewer than 100. A 1993 poll
done by the Times-Mirror Center for the People and the
Press found that almost half the adult population listened to talk radio. Only 27 percent of the listeners
voted for Clinton.

As the campaign drew to a close, the attacks grew
nastier. Oliver North, seeking a Senate seat, called
Washington "Sodom on the Potomac." T-shirts available
at the Virginia Republican convention read: WHERE IS
LEE HARVEY OSWALD WHEN AMERICA REALLY NEEDS HIM? But
it was Rush Limbaugh who had his eyes on the prize
and knew the only sure route to victory. He rallied his
faithful, the nearly twenty million he claims hear him
each week: "This is not the time to be depressed. This is
the time to remember the weapon that you have, and
that is the vote."

I watched the November 8 election returns late into the
night in my Boston hotel room. I had to leave Alabama

before the polls opened—one of the few times I had failed to vote since college.

The Republicans had gained control of both houses of Congress. The earth had moved under the political landscape. I was concerned with the message it might send to the militia extremists we were tracking.

Early Saturday morning after I returned home, I saddled Chico, my deep-red quarter horse, took him around the small barn pasture a few times to test his spirits, and turned south for the rolling hills and scattered moss-covered water oaks that lead to the flat pasture bordering Catoma Creek swamp. It was freezing when I left Boston, but the sixty-five-degree morning air barely kept Chico from breaking lather as I cantered him across the fields awash in golds and purples from goldenrods and ironweeds. I rode east directly toward the rising sun, zipped my jacket against the cool air, and thought about what had just transpired in the voting booth.

A Times-Mirror poll I had read in late September concluded that there was "no clear direction in the public's political thinking other than frustration with the current system." The electorate, the poll found, "was angry, self-absorbed and politically unanchored." The issues disturbing voters centered on race and on the role of the government.

Over half of the 3,800 polled agreed that equal rights had been pushed too far, up nearly ten points in less than two years. In 1971, 71 percent had said it was the responsibility of government to take care of people who cannot take care of themselves; only 57 percent agreed in the 1994 study. These voters, the poll found, had abandoned the Democratic Party in droves and were not sympathetic to blacks.

I knew that no Democratic presidential candidate

since Lyndon Johnson had won a majority of white voters. It was President Johnson who said in 1965 when he signed the Voting Rights Act enfranchising millions of blacks that it would be the death knell for the Democrats. "[T]o many white voters, the Democrats now look sufficiently 'black' to make them think twice about supporting its candidates," wrote Queens College political science professor Andrew Hacker in his 1992 bestseller, *Two Nations*. "The Republicans have been happy to build on these beliefs."

The Times-Mirror study confirmed the results of Republican efforts to win white votes, from Nixon's southern strategy to Bush's Willie Horton television commercials to the Gingrich Contract with America. The blatant racist rhetoric of Jesse Helms and George Wallace had been replaced with equally racist but more acceptable code words like welfare, affirmative action, reverse discrimination, and inner-city crime.

When southeast Los Angeles rioted after four policemen were acquitted of beating Rodney King, the rage was black, but the fear was white. This dramatic backdrop for the 1994 elections provided frightened whites with front-row seats to images of black-led larceny, arson, and murder.

The country was already choosing sides for the upcoming O. J. Simpson trial. Early polls showed about 70 percent of whites thought he was guilty; an equal percentage of blacks believed he was innocent. The whites and blacks were exposed to the same news reports but saw them through different eyes.

Pretrial surveys conducted by Jo-Ellan Dimitrius, the juristic psychologist employed by Simpson's defense team, showed that the jury pool was deeply divided along racial lines. A lot of issues unrelated to who murdered Ron Goldman and Nicole Brown Simpson would influence the verdict. The sixty-page jury questionnaire Dimitrius prepared would seek information to exploit these issues. Conservative politicians had already done it, first with divisive television ads, and then with a resounding victory at the polls.

Most whites, as Andrew Hacker has observed, see the country as "beset with racial problems they feel are not of their making." They feel they "bear neither responsibility nor blame for the conditions blacks face." Hacker observed, "Most white Americans believe that for at least the last generation blacks have been given more than a fair chance and at least equal opportunity if not outright advantage. About the only sacrifices on behalf of the nation's black minority these whites will agree to is for more police and prisons."

I remember the Republican television ads in the 1980s aimed at southern whites whose parents and grandparents had been lifelong Democrats. Two young, white, working-class men gather on the porch of a humble frame house to discuss politics. "I didn't leave the Democratic Party," one said, "they left me." The message: I haven't changed. The Democrats went after the black vote. I am not one of "them."

I rode past two white men servicing grass cutters for the day's mowing. I knew them and their families well. We had been to many church suppers together, and just the weekend before, I had seen them at the annual Pike Road Flea Market held in a century-old farmhouse donated to the community by a local rancher. My mother and wife were on the food committee, and I helped park some of the cars that came from miles around for this popular event. Few blacks attended.

I stopped Chico for a few minutes to pass the time of day with the tractor drivers, but I did not discuss the election. I already knew what they thought. The whites in the Pike Road precinct voted almost 100 percent Republican. The blacks all voted Democratic. Everything had changed in my community and in America since the civil rights movement, but by the same token, nothing had changed. As I watched my two neighbors climb on their tractors, I was angry at politicians, talk show hosts, and religious zealots who had fanned the flames of prejudice and fear.

I believe race was the underlying issue that accounted for the Republican victory. "Tax-and-spend Democrats" were blamed for the huge deficit. This translates to spending on social programs, welfare, and aid to minorities. Gun control critics played on the fear of black criminals, and immigration opponents saw incoming hordes of nonwhites.

I stopped my horse under a grove of trees that once shaded a tenant house on my great-uncle's cotton plantation.

It is one of my favorite spots, on a hill overlooking a lake with a large beaver mound along its western shore. About two dozen migrating mallards were swimming near the center. The closest home is more than a mile away, and the silence here has a noise of its own. I leaned against an old pecan tree as Chico picked at early clover shoots. The election was bad enough, I thought, but what effect would it have on the militia movement?

Would the militants who gathered at Estes Park and people like John Trochmann and Mark Koernke see the election as a license to encourage serious trouble?

They had seen Congressman Steve Stockman of Texas taken in by rumors of a nationwide military assault on militias, causing him to write Attorney General Reno about the "impending raid" and warning her that the attack would "run the risk of an irreparable

breach between the federal government and the public."
He accused President Clinton of staging the fatal
Branch Davidian episode to build support for an assault
weapons ban.

Newly elected Republican Representative Helen
Chenoweth of Idaho had become the darling of the
racist militia element when she proclaimed "white
Anglo-Saxon male[s] . . . are endangered." Her support
of Wise Use's environmental concerns locked in another
large militia constituency.

Militias now had influential friends in high places
and, in their view, a public mandate for radical change.
Would this embolden some of their less stable, trigger-
happy followers to speed up the revolution by taking
matters into their own hands?

George Wallace stood in the schoolhouse door to
block integration, and he castigated federal judges for
enforcing the law. His example surely inspired those
who bombed black churches and lynched civil rights
workers. Would the words of Chenoweth or Stockman
likewise encourage violence?

I knew we were on to something important with
our discovery of far-right extremists like Louis Beam
and Pete Peters manipulating the militias. I also knew
the public and even the Justice Department did not
fully share our concern. The response to my letter to
Reno had been disappointing. There had been a few
good investigative pieces by local writers, but the
major networks and newspapers were not tuned in.
The Center had launched its Militia Task Force, but I
was not sure our supporters appreciated the danger we
were tracking.

I felt something awful could happen that might
injure a lot of innocent people. When we took Louis
Beam to court and when we prosecuted Glenn Miller, I

had gotten a firsthand look at their violent plans and the propaganda they used to inspire their followers. Only a lucky break allowed the FBI to stop The Order before they bombed the 1984 Olympics in Los Angeles or assassinated a long list of prominent citizens. We might not be as fortunate this time.

To help alert the public to the danger, I wrote our supporters the following letter on January 9, 1995.

*Dear Center Supporter:*

I would like to share with you a deep concern I have about our country.

I am not concerned that a different political party now controls Congress. Voters have sent strong messages of dissatisfaction in mid-term elections for decades. What concerns me is the mean spirit in the message of the victors.

You know the types, critical of everything, impossible to please, incapable of compromise. They rule by fear and ridicule. Some come close to urging armed rebellion to "rescue" our country from the "enemy within."

Newt Gingrich, Jesse Helms, Strom Thurmond and others preach mistrust of our government. Soon they will be making policy decisions. I fear that unsophisticated and less tolerant people will see this hatred of government as a green light to cause serious trouble.

One of those angry and misguided citizens is John Trochmann, a white supremacist and founder of the new Militia of Montana. In a thinly veiled warning, he recently stated that "we don't want to go to the cartridge box [to take back our country]; but we will if we have to."

Intelligence agents in the Klanwatch division of

our Southern Poverty Law Center tell us that similar unauthorized militias now operate in at least eighteen states. Known white supremacists are filling leadership roles.

What really concerns me is that these misguided extremists believe our newly elected leaders approve of their twisted views, and that these extremists will now encourage other angry citizens to take matters into their own hands.

We recently established a Militia Task Force to monitor this growing armed citizen movement.

On a broader scale, we saw an increasing number of hate crimes committed in 1994 by ordinary citizens unconnected with hate groups. Radio talk show hosts, who promoted Newt Gingrich and his friends, daily spew out intolerance of anyone or anything unlike themselves.

I believe this is motivating angry people to vent their hostilities through rudeness and even violence.

*Morris Dees*
*Rolling Hills Ranch*

Two months after I wrote that letter, our Militia Task Force invited more than two dozen federal, state, and local law enforcement officers from around the country for a conference on the militias.

Essentially, we wanted to establish a network among those who tracked the extremist right to share the information our Militia Task Force was gathering and to get a better handle on how the militia movement was operating. We also wanted to share our concern that the militia movement posed a terrible threat to the country.

We discussed the striking similarities between today's militias and Louis Beam's Texas Emergency

Reserve and Glenn Miller's White Patriot Party. We went over carefully the speeches Pastor Pete Peters, Beam, and the other speakers had given at the Estes Park meeting. We listened to selected tapes of their talks. We also studied in detail the disturbing militia-related criminal incidents around the country.

In Virginia, four members of the Blue Ridge Hunt Club, including its founder James Roy Mullins, had been arrested on a variety of weapons charges, including the possession and sale of a short-barreled rifle and unregistered silencers, and facilitating the unlawful purchase of a firearm.

The group's members said they had formed their militia-like organization in order to lobby against gun control laws more effectively. Federal law enforcement officials, however, weren't convinced. In a search of Mullins's home and a separate warehouse, agents found thirteen guns, some with homemade silencers, explosives, hand grenades, and fuses and blasting caps. They also uncovered a plan to further arm the group by burglarizing the National Guard Armory in Pulaski, Virginia.

Federal agents also found a computer disk, which contained the draft of a newsletter article that outlined the group's goals. Authored by Mullins, the draft read in part:

> "Hit and run tactics will be our method of fighting. . . . We will destroy targets such as telephone relay centers, bridges, fuel storage tanks, communication towers, radio stations, airports. . . . Human targets will be engaged when it is beneficial to the cause to eliminate particular individuals who oppose us (troops, police, political figures, snitches . . . )."

Officials on the scene insisted this was no lobbying group. "Mullins is organizing a group of confederates, to be armed and trained in paramilitary fashion, in preparation for armed conflict with government authorities should firearms legislation become too restrictive," said one federal agent.

Police in Fowlerville, Michigan, expected to find a drunk driver when they stopped a car that was weaving across the road during the early morning hours of September 8, 1994. Instead, they found three men dressed in camouflage, their faces blackened, who identified themselves as members of the Michigan Militia and part of Mark Koernke's security team.

Police also discovered three semiautomatic 9mm pistols, a .357 Magnum revolver, an AK-47 assault rifle, an M1 rifle, an M14, seven hundred rounds of ammunition, three gas masks, night-vision binoculars, and handwritten notes that indicated the occupants of the vehicle were conducting night surveillance of local police departments.

The encounter left Fowlerville police chief Gary Krause a bit unnerved.

"They called cops 'punks in badges,' and said the next time one of them was stopped, they'd shoot the cop," he said at the time. "As far as I'm concerned they are a radical organization. I see them going in the direction of the Posse Comitatus. They see a one-world order coming with NATO. They're doing surveillance and reconnaisance of police departments and communication facilities.

"I think all cops should be leery now."

Still later in September, Missouri state trooper Bobbie Harper was shot in his home by a sniper armed with a high-powered rifle following a raid on the compound of the paramilitary group Citizens for Christ, led by Bob Joos, an Identity adherent. During the raid, police had found and seized a large quantity of dynamite, electric blasting caps, machine guns, and ammunition at the compound.

Harper was the officer who maced and arrested Joos during the raid. The suspect in the shooting was a member of Joos's group.

And just about the time the conference on militias started, John Trochmann and six associates were arrested in Roundup, Montana, some four hundred miles from Noxon, after the police there discovered they were carrying concealed weapons. The men were charged with felony syndicalism, the crime of being a "member of an organization that advocates crime, violence, damage to property, or unlawful means of terrorism for industrial or political ends."

At the time of the arrest, the police seized two dozen handguns and rifles, two-way radios and $28,000 in cash, 150 one-ounce gold coins valued at $57,000, and 200 silver coins.

Trochmann and the others disputed the charges. The Montana attorney general's office later dropped the case after it decided it was too weak to prosecute.

We stressed that law enforcement would likely see more militia-related criminal acts as the number of militias multiplied. In light of the militias' fierce antigovernment rhetoric, we explained that we saw government officials and facilities as likely targets. We urged those in attendance to convince their colleagues across the country not to buy the militia's line that their training was only defensive.

After our March conference on the militias, we turned our attention to planning for April. The influential Militia of Montana was attempting to make April 19 a red-letter date for the militia movement. It devoted almost the entire March issue of its newsletter, *Taking Aim*, to the case of Richard Wayne Snell, an Arkansas white supremacist convicted of two murders, who was scheduled to be executed on April 19, 1995.

Calling Snell a "Patriot to be Executed by The Beast," MOM linked his execution date to the April 19, 1993, burning of the Branch Davidian compound in Waco, Texas, and, erroneously, to the government's attempt to arrest white separatist Randy Weaver (the showdown at Ruby Ridge actually began on August 21, 1992), and to the burning of Lexington by British troops in 1776 (actually, the British burned military supplies in Concord on another April day of that year).

MOM claimed that April 19 was "the first day of a week-long sacrificial preparation for the GRAND CLIMAX ceremony celebrated by those who follow the Luciferian religion." It would join with others to call for the day to be nationally recognized as Militia Day.

Snell's pending execution, the incineration of the Branch Davidians, and the killing of Vicki and Samuel Weaver had become battle cries against the federal government that were sounded repeatedly at patriot and militia meetings, and in their faxes, flyers, newsletters, and Internet postings. At Snell's hearing before the Arkansas clemency board, one of his supporters warned board members and the governor that the "wrath of God" would fall upon them if Snell was executed as scheduled on April 19.

We didn't know what would happen on April 19, but we felt certain that something significant would occur. We learned that a group called the Veterans Against the New World Order with strong Identity leanings was planning an event to commemorate Waco and to protest Snell's execution at a Confederate memorial park in western Arkansas on April 19.

That morning, Mike Reynolds, one of our Militia Task Force investigators, boarded a plane to go there. It was 7:00 A.M. In Oklahoma City, parents were already dropping their children off at the day care center in the Alfred P. Murrah Federal Building.

# The Return of Earl Turner

It was only 10:30 in the morning on April 19, 1995, and I was already tired when I returned to my hotel room to collect my legal files and my suitcase for the drive back to Montgomery, Alabama.

The grind of the just-concluded, three-day deposition, combined with the almost unbearable humidity in the Florida panhandle, left me as limp as the paper in my notebook.

Two associates from the Southern Poverty Law Center and I had traveled to Navarre Beach, Florida, to depose John Burt, a militant antiabortion activist and the director of Our Father's House, a home for unwed mothers near Pensacola. Our civil suit claimed Burt had been involved in a conspiracy to stop abortions from being performed, through violent means if necessary, with a man named Michael Griffin. Griffin had been convicted the year before of assassinating Dr. David Gunn as he arrived at the rear door of the Women's Medical Services, an abortion clinic in Pensacola. In a civil lawsuit, Burt could be held liable for the doctor's death, if we could prove that the killing was a foreseeable consequence of the conspiracy. Our job at the deposition was to close the distance between Burt and Gunn's killer to allow a jury to find him liable for his actions as the motivator or coconspirator.

The deposition had gone well. So while I was tired and looked forward to going home, I also felt good.

As I closed the hotel room door, the sound of children at play in the swimming pool just a floor below me was replaced by the sharp jangle of the telephone.

I tossed my notebook on the bed and grabbed the receiver.

"Turn on the news," Joe Roy, one of my associates, said tersely. "I'll be right there."

I hung up the telephone, grabbed the remote control, and punched on the news channel.

"Oklahoma City was devastated this morning by a massive bomb that virtually destroyed a downtown federal building," said the television anchor.

The announcer seemed in shock as he narrated the video uplinked from a local station. Cars burning in the streets. Firemen, policemen, and citizens running into the smoldering remains of the building, bringing out victims. Some were small, bleeding children.

I just stood in front of the television. I found it hard to believe what I was seeing.

The squeals and screams of the children in the hotel's swimming pool magnified the horror of what I saw on the screen, as Joe Roy entered the room with a baggage cart. He placed my suitcase on the cart and then sat on the edge of the bed.

"They're saying it might be Mideast terrorists," he said, "like those who blew up the World Trade Center."

I nodded.

"I think the bad guys are a lot closer to home," Joe

added. "I think they should add some of the militia folks we've been tracking to their list of suspects."

Joe was the chief investigator for the Center's Klanwatch Project and its newly formed Militia Task Force. A former robbery-homicide detective with the Montgomery Police Department, he did not believe in coincidences. And, in his view, there were just too damn many of them in relation to the bombing.

The biggest of those coincidences was, of course, the date, April 19. Joe reminded me that we had sent Mike Reynolds to cover the Identity rally held to commemorate the two-year anniversary of the Waco debacle and to protest Richard Snell's execution.

There also was something eerily familiar about the bombing of the Alfred P. Murrah Federal Building.

In his 1978 novel, *The Turner Diaries*, William Pierce, a former college physics professor and now leader of the virulently racist and anti-Semitic National Alliance, describes how a group of white supremacists uses a truck bomb to blow up a federal building on the morning of October 13, 1990. The bombing leaves more than seven hundred people dead and signals the start of an eight-year guerrilla war against ZOG. During the war, federal officials, Jews, and minorities are killed, public facilities and synagogues are destroyed, and municipal water supplies are poisoned. Finally, in 1999, the liberation of North America was completed and the "dream of a White world became a certainty."

Although the book cannot be found in bookstores, more than two hundred thousand copies of *The Turner Diaries* have been sold to an underground army of believers, some of whom have used it as a guide for robbery, arson, assassination, and mass murder. Pierce sells the book as a "Blueprint," a "Handbook for White

Victory." He suggests that the faithful send a copy to any "friend who needs our message."

William Pierce is not simply an anti-Semite with a poison pen. He is a committed fascist. After a brief stint with the John Birch Society, he joined the leadership of the American Nazi Party in 1966 under George Lincoln Rockwell. Shortly after Rockwell's death, Pierce joined the National Youth Alliance. The mottos that summed up the group's philosophy were printed at the bottom of its stationery: "Free Men Are Not Equal" and "Equal Men Are Not Free."

In 1974, Pierce founded the National Alliance, his current organization. His group is committed to doing "whatever is necessary to achieve [a] White living space and to keep it White." It "will not be deterred by the difficulty or temporary unpleasantness involved." The type of "unpleasantness" from which Pierce will not shirk is reflected in the following passage from his membership bulletin.

> All the homosexuals, race mixers, and hard-case collaborators in the country who are too far gone to be re-educated can be rounded up, packed into 10,000 or so railroad cattle cars, and eventually double-timed into an abandoned coal mine in a few days time.

His group calls for "a long-term eugenics program."

Once Aryans attain total control and the country is purged of nonwhites, those who remain still will not have an equal voice. As Pierce explains in his statement of the "ideology and program" of the National Alliance:

> In the long run, . . . we want an honest government, not one which hides behind the carefully managed illusion that tens of millions of voters are its real

rulers. A government of and by politicians is not only grossly inefficient, it remains too susceptible to corruption and subversion, regardless of who controls the organs of public opinion. . . .

We need a government of men and women . . . whose attitude toward its mission is essentially *religious*: a government more like a holy order than like any existing secular government today. . . . The most important single institution in the government we want will be the one which selects, trains, and tests the people who will be the judges and the legislators and the executives in that government: people who will be more like *secular priests* in their behavior and their attitude toward their work than like today's politicians and bureaucrats.

In his 1995 review of the book for the *Village Voice*, Michael Tolkin wrote, "I want Jews to read this, because *The Turner Diaries* is a more horrifying book than *Mein Kampf*, and might come true in the same way.

"Reading Hitler, the shock is not so much the book in itself—there's a basic incoherence to *Mein Kampf*, but everything that came afterward was there for the world to see, so reading *The Turner Diaries*, one can't pretend that it can't happen here."

It was in the early 1980s, through my work as chief trial counsel for the Southern Poverty Law Center, that I first encountered militia fanatics who saw the book as prophecy and used its gruesome tale of genocide to justify criminal acts in the name of a holy crusade to save their race.

One of those fanatics was Robert Mathews.

On a chilly September evening in 1983, Robert Mathews led the eight "Aryan kinsmen" to the bunkhouse that sat adjacent to his home in the Selkirk Mountains outside of Metaline Falls, Washington. Once inside, the men negotiated the tight stairway to the second floor where lit candles surrounded a blanket spread out on the floor. The flames of the candles flickered furiously, casting eerily large shadows all about the drafty, sparsely furnished room.

Mathews directed the men to form a circle around the blanket. As they did, one of the men placed his six-week-old daughter on the blanket. Mathews then asked the men to join hands and repeat an oath he recited.

"I, as a free Aryan man, hereby swear an unrelenting oath upon the green graves of our sires, upon the children in the wombs of our wives, upon the throne of God almighty, sacred is His name, to join together in holy union with those brothers in this circle and to declare forthright that from this moment on I have no fear of death, no fear of foe; that I have a sacred duty to do whatever is necessary to deliver our people from the Jew and bring total victory to the Aryan race.

"I, as an Aryan warrior, swear myself to complete secrecy to The Order and total loyalty to my comrades."

The men vowed that should one of them be killed in battle, the others would care for that man's family and avenge his death by tracking down the killer and removing his head from his body. They also vowed that should one of them be taken prisoner, the others would do whatever was necessary to free him.

"And furthermore," they continued, "let me bear witness to you, my brothers, that if I break this oath, let me be forever cursed upon the lips of our people as a coward and an oath breaker.

"My brothers, let us be His battle ax and weapons of war. Let us go forth by ones and by twos, by scores and by legions, and as true Aryan men with pure hearts and strong minds face the enemies of our faith and our race with courage and determination.

"We hereby invoke the blood covenant and declare that we are in a full state of war and will not lay down our weapons until we have driven the enemy into the sea and reclaimed the land which was promised to our fathers of old, and through our blood and His will, becomes the land of our children to be."

So began The Order, which, over the next eighteen months, would become one of the most violent and daring paramilitary forces ever unleashed on America by the far-right extremist movement.

For Robert Mathews, the formation of The Order represented an end to all the talk that had consumed his life during his twenty-year odyssey through the far-right extremes of American politics. As an eleven-year-old, he joined the John Birch Society and heard talk of the need to steel America against Communist infiltration and takeover. As a member of an Arizona tax protest group, Mathews heard talk that the income tax was the second plank of the Communist manifesto and that the Federal Reserve had placed control of the country's money and credit into the hands of private, Jewish bankers. As an associate of Richard Butler's Aryan Nations and William Pierce's National Alliance, he heard talk of the need for a revolution to save the white race.

Mathews became convinced that a "great sickness" had overcome the country.

"It is self-evident to all who have eyes to see that an evil shadow has fallen across our once fair land," he wrote in what eventually would become his Declaration of War against ZOG. "Evidence abounds that a certain vile, alien people have taken control over our people.

"All about us the land is dying. Our cities swarm

with dusky hordes, the water is rancid and the air is rank. Our farms are being seized by usurious leeches and our people are being forced off the land. The capitalists and the communists pick gleefully at our bones while the vile hook-nosed masters of usury orchestrate our destruction."

Mathews complained that the country's rich had so tightened the chains on the white working class that it was now composed of a pitiful, dispossessed people.

"[The rich] close the factories, the mills, the mines, and ship our jobs overseas," wrote Mathews. "They send an army of agents into our midst to steal from our pockets and enforce their rule. Our forefathers under King George knew freedom more than we. Yet still, still, our people sleep."

No longer, declared Mathews. It was now time for action. "By ones and by twos, by scores and by legions we will drive the enemy into the sea. Through our blood and God's will, the land promised to our fathers of old will become the land of our children to be," he vowed.

His blueprint for the white revolution was *The Turner Diaries*. He gave a copy to each member of The Order to study.

The opening shots of Mathews's revolution were fired in October 1983 with the armed robbery of a pornographic bookstore in Spokane, Washington. Mathews and three of his confederates escaped with $369. The take barely covered their expenses, let alone help finance a revolution.

But with each subsequent robbery, Mathews and The Order, which grew to more than two dozen members, became more polished, more professional.

In December 1983, Mathews robbed a bank north of Seattle of nearly $26,000. Then in March 1984, Mathews and three members of The Order escaped with $43,000 after robbing a store in a Seattle mall. A month later, the group hit an armored car in a second Seattle mall and made off with more than $500,000. Their masterpiece, however, occurred in July 1984, when Mathews and a force of fifteen Order members stole more than $3.8 million from an armored car outside of Ukiah, California.

Only $600,000 of the nearly $4.3 million stolen in the robberies has ever been recovered. Authorities believe that Mathews distributed the remaining millions to a host of white supremacist leaders, including Louis Beam and Richard Butler.

William Pierce, according to information supplied to federal authorities, received some of the robbery loot in appreciation for his having written *The Turner Diaries*. (Pierce denies he got any money.) Mathews had been a loyal member of Pierce's organization, the National Alliance. In a talk that Pierce said was "well received by the Alliance members," at one of their conferences, Mathews reminded Pierce's followers:

> The fate of every last white man, woman and child on this planet lies squarely on the shoulders of us here in this room today. . . . So, kinsmen, duty calls. The future is now. If months from now you have not yet fully committed yourself to the Alliance and the responsibilities thereof, then you have in effect not only betrayed your race, you have betrayed yourself. So, stand up like men! And drive the enemy into the sea!

Like Earl Turner and his compatriots in *The Turner Diaries*, Mathews and his comrades engaged in counterfeiting as a means to wreck the economy and undermine ZOG.

And like Earl Turner and his compatriots, the members of The Order engaged in murder. The Order's first victim was one of their own, Walter West, whom they suspected of betraying them. Then, on June 18, 1984, Order members gunned down Jewish talk show host Alan Berg outside his Denver home. Berg was one of several enemies Mathews and his band of terrorists targeted for assassination. Because of my ongoing battle with Louis Beam, I also was at the top of their list. Killing me was not enough for Mathews. His animus was so great that he told one of his supporters, Thomas Martinez, that "we're going to kidnap [Dees] and then we'll torture him and get as much information out of him as we can, and when we have that, we'll kill him, and bury him and pour lye over him."

The Order's revolution ended on December 8, 1984. After being betrayed to the FBI by Martinez, Mathews was tracked down on Whidbey Island, north of Seattle. There, he was killed in a hail of bullets and fire after barricading himself in his island hideout against an assault by federal and state law enforcement officers.

The remaining members of The Order were eventually captured and tried on multiple state and federal charges that included counterfeiting, armed robbery, conspiracy, and murder. In 1985, twenty-four members of the group were convicted or pleaded guilty. All were sentenced to long prison terms.

Following the death of the man who idolized him, Pierce said he had tried to steer Mathews away from armed confrontation with ZOG. "I told him . . . that white people, generally, weren't yet in a revolutionary mood," said Pierce.

Still, William Pierce had nothing but praise for Mathews.

"Bob gave us a very important symbol," said Pierce. "He did what was morally right. He may have been a bit premature . . . and he may have made many tactical errors. But he reminded us that we are not engaged in a debate between gentlemen.

"Instead, we are engaged in the most desperate war we have ever fought. A war for the survival of our race. . . . Ultimately we cannot win it except by killing our enemies . . . and we cannot kill our enemies without taking a chance on being killed ourselves."

It was a reminder, insisted Pierce, that every member of the Patriot movement needed.

"Bob elevated . . . our struggle. He took us from name-calling to blood-letting. He cleared the air for all. In the long run that will be helpful," said Pierce.


"I'll bet you good money the militia or white supremacists are involved in this," said Joe Roy as he rose from the bed, placed my briefcase on the baggage cart, and started to steer it into the hallway.

"I bet you're right," I said almost to myself, still unable to take my eyes off the television screen.

As Joe headed downstairs to pack the car for the trip home, I picked up the telephone and placed a call to Barry Kowalski, my quickest contact with the Justice Department and the FBI.

"Joe thinks it's the militia or some white supremacist group that's involved with the bombing," I told him.

Barry said he didn't have any information that contradicted Joe's hunch and thanked me for calling. "Keep me informed if you learn anything," he added just before hanging up.

I spent the three-hour ride from Pensacola to Montgomery making a to-do list for the case against Burt and, when possible, listening to the news about the bombing on the radio. Sketchy reports of a mounting death toll, possibly including dozens of children, came in news breaks that also included speculation about just who would commit such a horrific act. Although government officials refused to lay blame on a particular group, outside experts being interviewed stated that the signs pointed to Mideast terrorists. Joe continued to point to home-grown terrorists who took a page out of *The Turner Diaries*.

I felt sick about the tragedy. The brief images I'd seen in my Holiday Inn room of burning cars and injured people were sobering reminders of how vulnerable the United States was to the types of terrorist attacks that had rocked other parts of the world so frequently. The World Trade Center bombing was still fresh in my mind. It had been so easy to drive a bomb-filled van into the basement. How could our open society protect itself from zealots willing to kill innocent people in an ideological war? I didn't know for sure, of course, but I had a sinking feeling that Joe was right.

We arrived in Montgomery at about 2:00 P.M., and went directly to the Center. I checked my mail and then joined a number of my colleagues who were gathered around a television set. I brought with me a copy of *The Turner Diaries*.

As we watched the tragic drama that was still unfolding in Oklahoma City, I opened the book to the chapter describing the bombing of the federal building.

"At 9:15 yesterday morning our bomb went off in the FBI's national headquarters building. Our worries about the relatively small size of the bomb were unfounded; the damage is immense," began the chapter.

> The scene in the courtyard was one of utter devastation. The whole Pennsylvania Avenue wing of the building, as we could then see, had collapsed, partly

into the courtyard in the center of the building and partly into Pennsylvania Avenue. A huge, gaping hole yawned in the courtyard pavement just beyond the rubble of collapsed masonry, and it was from this hole that most of the column of black smoke was ascending.

Overturned trucks and automobiles, smashed office furniture, and building rubble were strewn wildly about—and so were the bodies of a shockingly large number of victims.

And then, just as we were doing at the Center, the characters in the book watched "the TV coverage of rescue crews bringing the dead and injured out of the building."

"It is a heavy burden of responsibility for us to bear since most of the victims of our bomb were only pawns who were no more committed to the sick philosophy or the racially destructive goals of the System than we are," said the book's central character, Earl Turner. "But there is no way we can destroy the System without hurting many thousands of innocent people—no way. It is a cancer too deeply rooted in our flesh. And if we don't destroy the System before it destroys us—if we don't cut this cancer out of our living flesh—our whole race will die."

I closed the book. I had read enough to feel even more strongly that Joe was right. I felt certain that real-life Earl Turners were involved in the Oklahoma City bombing.

# The Almost Perfect Soldier

At 10:20 A.M. on Wednesday, April 19—as the dead, dying, and dazed were being hauled out of the rubble of what was once the Alfred P. Murrah Federal Building— Oklahoma state trooper Charles Hanger noticed a 1977 yellow Mercury Marquis traveling north on Interstate 35. The car had no license plate.

Hanger pulled the vehicle over just outside of Billings, some sixty miles north of Oklahoma City. As the driver reached for his wallet, Hanger saw a bulge under the man's jacket. The trooper drew his service revolver and asked the man what he had under his coat. It was a 9mm Glock semiautomatic pistol loaded with Black Talon bullets called "cop killers" because they can penetrate body armor.

The driver, who said his name was Timothy McVeigh, insisted the gun was just for self-protection as he drove cross-country. Hanger was suspicious. McVeigh had no luggage, something Hanger would expect to find on such a long trip. The trooper ordered him out of the car and placed him under arrest on charges of carrying a concealed weapon, transporting a loaded gun, and for driving without a license plate and insurance. Hanger then placed McVeigh in his patrol car and took him to the county jail in Perry, Oklahoma. During the trip to Perry, Hanger told McVeigh that there had been a massive explosion in Oklahoma City, but that authorities had yet to determine its cause. The trooper would be going back that way once he dropped off McVeigh at the jail.

In most cases involving misdemeanor charges, the person is arraigned and then released on bond, usually within twenty-four hours. But this time, Judge Dan Allen was busy with a divorce case and the arraignment had to be postponed. McVeigh would have to stay in jail until a hearing could be scheduled. He offered no argument against the delay. He would wait.

That compliant attitude was just like the Timothy McVeigh friends, acquaintances, and employers knew.

"Timmy just wasn't the type of person who could initiate action," Lynda Haner-Mele, McVeigh's supervisor when he worked for Burns International Security Services in Kenmore, New York, told a *New York Times* reporter. "He was very good if you said 'Tim, watch this door—don't let anyone through.'"

Timothy McVeigh was born in Pendleton, New York.

By most accounts, including his own, McVeigh had an ordinary childhood. Although his parents divorced when he was ten, McVeigh claimed it didn't have an impact on him. Friends, however, said he never had a kind word for his mother. "I just remember him calling his momma 'that no-good whore, a slut' words like that," said John Kelso, who was an army buddy of McVeigh's.

When his mother Mildred moved to Florida with one of his two sisters, McVeigh stayed with his father William. While growing up, he helped in his father's vegetable garden, dabbled in high school sports, worked at a fast-food place, and avoided cliques.

"He hung out with a lot of varieties, honor students, different friends," said classmate Charles Brennan. "He was the type of person who hung out with everyone."

After graduation, McVeigh studied briefly at a business college but became bored with the routine and the classes.

The classroom was no match for the shooting range McVeigh had created on a ten-acre plot of land he owned with his friend Dave Darlak. While Darlak's interest in the range waned, McVeigh's only seemed to grow. He wanted to be out there every weekend. He camped overnight, shot all day.

After he quit college, McVeigh got a job with an armored car company, Burke Armor, Inc. He took his passion for guns off the shooting range and brought it to the job.

One day he showed up for work with a sawed-off shotgun and bandoliers slung in an $X$ over his chest. "He came to work looking like Rambo," his partner of eight months, Jeff Camp, recounted. "It looked like World War III."

When his supervisor told McVeigh that he couldn't go out on the truck dressed like "Rambo," he got angry.

Not long after that incident, McVeigh found a home for his passion for guns. In May 1988, he joined the U.S. Army and was assigned to Fort Benning, Georgia, for boot camp.

There he fashioned himself into an excellent soldier. "As far as soldiering, he never did anything wrong," an infantryman in McVeigh's company remembered. "He was always on time. He never got into trouble. He was perfect. He was always volunteering for stuff that the rest of us wouldn't want to do, guard duties, classes on weekends."

At Fort Benning, McVeigh met Terry Nichols, who shared McVeigh's love for weapons and many of his political views. The two men became fast friends. That friendship was interrupted when McVeigh and Nichols were assigned to different companies at Fort Riley, Kansas, after basic training, and when Nichols left the military due to a family emergency a few months later.

At Fort Riley, McVeigh was a gunner on a Bradley fighting vehicle in the Second Battalion, a mechanized infantry unit. He continued to excel as a soldier. He was quickly promoted to corporal, then sergeant, and became the best shot among the sixty-five 25mm cannon gunners in his battalion.

He also began to develop another passion. An avid reader of *Soldier of Fortune* and other gun-related magazines, McVeigh became enamored with the writings of extremist-right authors. For his news, McVeigh favored *Spotlight*, the newsletter of the anti-Semitic Liberty Lobby, and *Patriot Report*, an Arkansas-based Christian Identity newsletter, over more mainstream fare. And then there was *The Turner Diaries*, his favorite book. It was his bible, said friends.

McVeigh also developed a fascination with Hitler. That fascination cost him at least one relationship, perhaps the only relationship McVeigh had with a woman, said friends.

"From what I remember, he said he didn't necessarily agree with all those Jews being killed," recalled Catina Lawson. "But he said Hitler had the right plan. I think he was talking about when Hitler tried to conquer the world, how he went about it, little pieces at a time.

He thought that was admirable. I didn't like him after that."

McVeigh's hatred for African-Americans also cost him. He often assigned blacks the "dirty" details and frequently used the word "nigger" and other racist terms. His racism resulted in a reprimand after blacks in his unit complained. It was the only blemish on his otherwise sterling military record.

In January 1991, just prior to the start of Desert Storm, McVeigh's unit was shipped to the Persian Gulf. Comrades recalled that McVeigh was excited about going to war and that following the conflict, he boasted of shooting an Iraqi soldier in the head from a distance of 1,100 meters. McVeigh downplayed the incident. "There was only a single shot fired on that first day," he said, "and that was to get them to come out of [their bunkers]."

Following the war, which ended four days and four hours after it began, McVeigh returned to the United States to begin training for the Green Berets. But two days into the twenty-one-day qualification program, McVeigh withdrew. News accounts have suggested that he washed out because he failed a psychological test and that he was extremely upset by it. "That's a bunch of bunk," McVeigh recalled. "I had gotten new boots and blisters started to break out. Any realist knows that if you develop blisters on the second day . . . you're not going to make it."

Still, it wasn't long after that failure that the man everyone thought would be a career soldier opted for an early out. He returned to the Buffalo, New York, area, got a job as a security officer with Burns International Security Services, and joined the National Guard.

Like many who had hoped for so much yet achieved so little, McVeigh was bitter toward the government.

"He would talk about the government a lot," recalled his former girlfriend. "Usually the topic was brought up by him. He would shoot off his mouth and just bitch about the government."

McVeigh also believed a person had a right to do more than just bitch about the government. He saw violence as a legitimate option to convince the government to see the error of its ways. In a February 1992 letter to the *Union-Sun & Journal* in his hometown of Lockport, New York, that could have been written by thousands of similarly minded "Patriots" from around the country, McVeigh wrote:

> Crime is out of control. Criminals have no fear of punishment. Prisons are overcrowded so they know they will not be imprisoned long. . . .
>
> Taxes are a joke. Regardless of what a political candidate "promises," they will increase taxes. More taxes are always the answer to government misman-agement. . . .
>
> The "American Dream" of the middle class has all but disappeared, substituted with people struggling just to buy next week's groceries. Heaven forbid the car breaks down! . . .
>
> Politicians are out of control. Their yearly salaries are more than an average person will see in a life-time. They have been entrusted with the power to regulate their own salaries, and have grossly violated that trust to live in their own luxury. . . .
>
> Who is to blame for the mess? At a point when the world has seen communism falter as an imperfect system to manage people, democracy seems to be headed down the same road. No one is seeing the "big" picture. . . .
>
> What is it going to take to open up the eyes of our elected officials? AMERICA IS IN SERIOUS DECLINE.

We have no proverbial tea to dump; should we instead sink a ship full of Japanese imports? Is a Civil War imminent? Do we have to shed blood to reform the current system? I hope it doesn't come to that! But it might.

McVeigh was particularly alarmed about the direction of the U.S. military he had just left. "He wasn't happy about Somalia, that if we could put the United States under basically U.N. command and send them to Somalia to disarm their citizens, then why couldn't they come do the same thing in the United States," reflected Sergeant Albert Warnement, McVeigh's former commander on the Bradley fighting vehicle. Friends recounted that McVeigh was also concerned that military units were involved in drug enforcement along the U.S.-Mexican border and had been called out during the 1992 Los Angeles riots.

McVeigh had drifted into the Patriot and militia movement.

"He sent me a lot of newsletters and stuff from those groups he was involved in," recalled Warnement. "There were newsletters from Bo Gritz's group, some other odd newsletters, some from the Patriots; then he sent that videotape, *The Big Lie,* about Waco."

*The Big Lie* was produced by Indianapolis attorney Linda Thompson, the self-proclaimed head of the Unorganized Militia of the United States of America, who had protested against the government during the Waco siege. The half-hour video claims to show how the FBI deliberately set the fire that destroyed the Branch Davidian compound. A viewing staple among Patriot movement members, the video claims that a government tank spewed flames, not tear gas, into the main building.

Not long after Waco, McVeigh quit his security job and moved to Kingman, Arizona, where he bunked with an old army friend, Mike Fortier, who lived in a trailer park on the northeastern edge of town. Although he worked briefly at a hardware store there, authorities say McVeigh appeared to use the town more for a mail drop than a residence. He was constantly on the move.

There was a pilgrimage to Waco, where he visited the ruins of the Branch Davidian compound. In Decker, Michigan, he visited his old army buddy Terry Nichols and his brother James. There McVeigh experimented with demolitions and attended at least one meeting of the Michigan Militia with the Nichols brothers. James urged the group to go after judges, lawyers, and police officers, a view that didn't sit well with everyone in attendance. "These people had attempted to come to meetings and speak out," claimed Michigan Militia cofounder Norman Olson shortly after the Oklahoma City bombing, "but they were silenced. In fact, they were told to leave."

McVeigh also made repeated trips to gun shows throughout the country. At some, he set up a table and sold canteens and duffel bags. At others he sold baseball caps with the letters ATF surrounded by simulated bullet holes. There was one item he sold at all the events: *The Turner Diaries*.

"He carried that book all the time," one gun collector recalled. "He sold it at the shows. He'd have a few copies in the cargo pocket of his cammies. They were supposed to be $10, but he'd sell them for $5. It was like he was looking for converts."

Another gun dealer claimed McVeigh even slept with the book under his pillow.

On April 12, 1995, McVeigh headed east out of Kingman. It was a journey that would end with him sitting in a county jail in Perry, Oklahoma.

\*     \*     \*

Within hours of the bombing, investigators found the twisted remains of a truck axle two blocks east of the Murrah Building as McVeigh sat in the county jail. The axle's identification number—commonly stamped on major vehicle body parts to thwart thieves—led authorities to Ryder Rentals of Miami where they quickly learned the truck was assigned to Elliot's Body Shop in Junction City, Kansas, approximately 250 miles north of Oklahoma City.

After they interviewed the rental agent, federal agents determined that the name, address, and South Dakota driver's license provided by one of the two men who rented the truck were bogus.

The next morning, Thursday, April 20, the rental agent helped authorities create two composite drawings that were quickly disseminated to the news media and law enforcement officials. In Oklahoma City, three witnesses said one of the composites looked like a crew-cut man they had seen outside the entrance of the building just prior to the bombing. In Junction City, employees at the Dreamland Motel said the sketch resembled a man who had stayed there from April 14 to April 17. The man's name was Tim McVeigh. He was from Decker, Michigan. He drove an older-model Mercury.

A check of the Michigan Department of Motor Vehicles records uncovered a license issued to Timothy J. McVeigh of North Van Dyke Road, where James Nichols's farm was located.

On Friday, April 21, the FBI received a call from a man who had worked with McVeigh. He had recognized the composite on television. He told agents that McVeigh held extreme right-wing views and that he was "particularly agitated about the conduct of the federal government at Waco, Texas, in 1993."

The FBI entered McVeigh's Social Security number into the National Crime Information Center computer. A match came up with an arrest made in Oklahoma's Noble County. Agents contacted the sheriff's office and asked them to hold McVeigh, who was less than an hour away from being released.

After he was transferred from state to federal custody, McVeigh was flown to Tinker Air Force Base where he was arraigned on charges of blowing up the Oklahoma City federal building and ordered held without bail. He was then transported to the El Reno federal corrections facility outside of Oklahoma City.

In Herington, Kansas, Terry Nichols sat in his living room and watched news accounts of McVeigh's arrest. He rose from his chair, gave his wife some money, and left the house. He drove to the police station. "I think you are looking for me," he told them.

Nichols, too, was arrested, arraigned, and ordered held without bail.

On August 10, 1995, a federal grand jury indicted the two men—who both maintain their innocence—on charges ranging from conspiracy to murder in connection with the bombing that killed 169 people, wounded more than 500, and left a hole twenty feet wide and eight feet deep.

In the official-sounding words of the federal grand jury's indictment, Timothy James McVeigh and Terry Lynn Nichols committed and caused to be committed the following acts:

- On September 30, 1994, McVeigh and Nichols purchased forty fifty-pound bags of ammonium nitrate in McPherson, Kansas, under the name "Mike Havens."

- On October 1, 1994, McVeigh and Nichols stole explosives from a storage locker in Marion, Kansas.
- On October 3 & 4, 1994, McVeigh and Nichols transported the stolen explosives to Kingman, Arizona, and rented a storage unit for them.
- On October 18, 1994, McVeigh and Nichols purchased forty fifty-pound bags of ammonium nitrate in McPherson, Kansas, under the name "Mike Havens."
- In October of 1994, McVeigh and Nichols planned a robbery of a firearms dealer in Arkansas as a means to obtain moneys to help finance their planned act of violence.
- On November 5, 1994, McVeigh and Nichols caused firearms, ammunition, coins, United States currency, precious metals and other property to be stolen from a firearms dealer in Arkansas.
- On December 16, 1994, while en route to Kansas to take possession of firearms stolen in Arkansas robbery, McVeigh drove with Michael Fortier to the Alfred P. Murrah Building and identified the building as the target.
- In March of 1995, McVeigh obtained a driver's license in the name of "Robert Kling" bearing a date of birth of April 19, 1972.
- On April 14, 1995, McVeigh purchased a 1977 Mercury Marquis in Junction City, Kansas; called the Nichols residence in Herington, Kansas; called a business in Junction City and, using the name of "Bob Kling," inquired about renting a truck capable of carrying 5,000 pounds of cargo; and rented a motel room in Junction City.
- On April 15, 1995, McVeigh placed a deposit for a rental truck in the name of "Robert Kling."

- On April 17, 1995, McVeigh took possession of a 20-foot rental truck in Junction City, Kansas.
- On April 18, 1995, at Geary Lake State Park in Kansas, McVeigh and Nichols constructed an explosive truck bomb with barrels filled with a mixture of ammonium nitrate, fuel and other explosives placed in the cargo compartment of the rental truck.
- On April 19, 1995, McVeigh parked the truck bomb directly outside the Alfred P. Murrah Federal Building, located within the Western District of Oklahoma, during regular business and day-care hours.
- On April 19, 1995, McVeigh caused the truck bomb to explode.

What the bare bones language of the indictment does not disclose are the striking parallels between the Oklahoma City bombing and the bombing that is recounted in the pages of McVeigh's favorite book, *The Turner Diaries*.

In William Pierce's 1978 novel, a truck containing a "little under 5,000 pounds" of fuel oil and ammonium nitrate fertilizer is detonated at 9:15 A.M. in front of the FBI's Washington, D.C., headquarters. In Oklahoma City, a truck containing approximately 4,400 pounds of fuel oil and ammonium nitrate fertilizer is detonated at 9:05 A.M. in front of a federal building that houses the FBI and the ATF. The fictional bomb blows off the front of the building, causing the upper floors to collapse. In Oklahoma City, the bomb also caused the upper floors to collapse.

In *The Turner Diaries*, the bombing is sparked by the passage of a federal gun control act. Both McVeigh and Nichols are strongly opposed to gun control. The book's main character, Earl Turner, considers himself a "patriot," and is the member of an antigovernment underground cell that funds its operations by robbing banks. The two suspects in the Oklahoma City bombing consider themselves patriots, and the FBI believes both are members of an underground antigovernment cell. Turner was openly racist. So was McVeigh.

What the indictment also doesn't reveal is McVeigh's connections to the militia and the underground Patriot movement, many of whose members share his passion for the book. Given that the prosecutors need only show at trial that McVeigh and Nichols are guilty of the bombing—something the prosecutors may be able to do solely with scientific evidence, a few witnesses, and a paper trail—the public may never know all the conspirators or all who influenced McVeigh.

How extensive were McVeigh's connections with militia groups?

Florida militia members have claimed that a man who resembled McVeigh came with Michigan's Mark Koernke on an organizing tour. Koernke is one of the movement's most militant spokespersons. His three militia-related videotapes are owned by thousands and viewed by thousands more. In one of them he jokes about lynching public officials. Koernke denies knowing McVeigh. But an attorney for the cofounder of the Michigan Militia once stated that when he looked in his Rolodex for Koernke's telephone number, he found McVeigh listed as the contact. He later said the name was "Tim McKay," not "Tim McVeigh."

McVeigh did attend at least one Michigan Militia meeting where Koernke was in attendance. The cofounder of that group, Norman Olson, was quick to distance McVeigh from the group. He now claims they ejected McVeigh from the meeting.

When McVeigh was questioned by FBI agents prior to his obtaining a lawyer, he followed the code of conduct that members of the Michigan Militia, as well as members of other militia groups, swear to abide by if "captured" by federal authorities.

> I am bound to give only name, rank, and date of birth. I will evade answering further questions to the utmost of my ability. I will make no oral or written statements disloyal to my beloved homeland and its citizens or harmful to their continued struggle for liberty and freedom as prescribed in the Constitution of the United States.

McVeigh gave federal agents, according to news accounts, only his name, rank, and date of birth.

Did McVeigh, like Robert Mathews, have a relationship with *Turner Diaries* author William Pierce or his neo-Nazi National Alliance group?

Anyone can purchase *The Turner Diaries*. But McVeigh sold them in quantity at gun shows. He might have purchased multiple copies at a 1993 gun show in Kingman, Arizona, from the National Alliance booth. A sign above the booth, one that would have attracted a gun lover like McVeigh, read: WHAT WILL YOU DO WHEN THEY COME TO TAKE YOUR GUNS? Or he might have placed a bulk order with National Vanguard Books, located at William Pierce's Hillsboro, West Virginia, compound. No one knows for sure.

Authorities do know that McVeigh, using the name "Tim Tuttle," made at least seven telephone calls to a message center operated by the National Alliance. Recorded messages warn that the federal government could "face the wrath of an awakened and armed people."

Of course, anyone can call one of the twenty or so National Alliance message centers scattered across the country. But not everyone can call Pierce's unlisted number.

Two separate law enforcement sources told CNN that McVeigh's telephone records show that he placed a call to Pierce's unlisted number in West Virginia in the weeks before the bombing. They said it was a lengthy call. Pierce denies knowing or talking to McVeigh.

Did McVeigh work with a secret militia cell, one of the leaderless resistance types promoted by Louis Beam?

If McVeigh was the bomber, he did not work alone. Michael Fortier has admitted in a plea agreement that he helped McVeigh scout out the Alfred P. Murrah Federal Building. Terry Nichols allegedly helped him purchase and store the explosives. An unknown man robbed an Arkansas gun dealer of more than seventy weapons, gold and silver coins, and $8,700 in cash to finance the bomb plot. McVeigh reprinted copies of paramilitary publications at the K-Max copy center in Kingman, according to its owner George Boerst. He would not have needed extra copies unless, maybe, he was supplying them to his confederates.

McVeigh's connections to Elohim City, a far-right Christian Identity compound on the Arkansas-Oklahoma border, are highly suspicious. Reverend Robert Millar denies he knew McVeigh or that McVeigh visited the compound, but the telephone records show he called Elohim City on April 5, just two weeks before the bombing. He could have been looking for a place to hide after the blast. McVeigh was within ten miles of Elohim City on October 12, 1993. He was ticketed that day for a minor traffic offense by a local deputy sheriff on County Route 220, the only access road into the compound.

McVeigh might also have planned to mourn the death of Richard Snell at Elohim City. Reverend Millar brought Snell's body to the compound from the

Arkansas prison where this white supremacist hero was executed just a few hours after the government says McVeigh lit the fuse to the Ryder truck bomb. Millar's plans to bring the corpse to Elohim City were as well known in the Patriot movement as the significance of the date, April 19.

The driver's license McVeigh presented to Trooper Charles Hanger told volumes about his connections and priorities. His date of birth was listed as April 19, 1972. McVeigh was born on April 23, 1968.

McVeigh surely had a private laugh when he gave the clerk at the motor vehicle registry the bogus birth date. He also probably got a chuckle whenever he used the name "T. Tuttle." Tuttle was the last name of a terrorist played by Robert De Niro in the 1985 movie *Brazil*. In the movie, Tuttle set off a bomb that destroyed a building filled with government bureaucrats. McVeigh offered small clues to a big puzzle he never expected anyone to solve.

Even if McVeigh is convicted, we may never know who gave him his marching orders or if he himself led the troops. But I would be much more skeptical than the *New York Times*. On the day McVeigh and Nichols were indicted, the paper editorialized:

> In the end, this case may turn out to be much simpler than many had thought. At this point it looks like two former Army buddies, nursing hatred of the Government, carried out the most destructive act of domestic terrorism in the nation's history. That is reassuring in the sense that there may be no organized conspiracy in place to carry out other terrorist bombings.

McVeigh told the court he did not bomb the federal building. His lawyer was a bit more cautious when he

allowed *Newsweek* to interview McVeigh in an effort to
humanize him. He said that McVeigh would enter a not
guilty plea and would put the government to its proof at
trial.

I'm sure McVeigh's experienced defense lawyer,
Stephen Jones, is leaving a few options open in the
court of public opinion. He knows prospective jurors
will likely read what his client says. This is a serious
case involving the death penalty. Jones knows how it
feels to have a client executed. He knows that if the jury
finds McVeigh guilty, it will then retire to a second hearing to determine if his client should live or die. If they
convict McVeigh, Jones doesn't want the jury to have
remembered his client making elaborate denials to
*Newsweek*. Jurors despise a lying defendant. If McVeigh
does not testify, and he probably will not, and if he is
convicted, and I feel he probably will be, Jones can tell
the jury it was his duty to force the government to
prove its case. He will then hope that the jury will not
hold his strategy against his client as they consider mit-
igating evidence Jones might offer to avoid the death
penalty for McVeigh.

In the summer of 1995 the students at Gerry
Spence's Trial Lawyer's College, held at his Wyoming
ranch, chose the McVeigh case to practice how sea-
soned trial attorneys plan a defense. I was one of the
Old Warriors, as Gerry calls the volunteer faculty.

I suggested to the Young Warriors, fifty lawyers who
gave up a month from their practice to come, that, for
the purposes of our exercise, we presume McVeigh
guilty to eliminate a complicated factual defense based
on evidence we could not know. Many skilled trial
lawyers would not admit guilt, even if their client committed the act charged. In the McVeigh case, it might be
an especially risky strategy. A safer, more conservative

approach would be to attack the government's case at every turn, hoping to create reasonable doubt.

I have worked on more than fifty capital cases. Most of the defendants were clearly guilty. Some of the guilty ones had weak factual defenses. Winning these cases, though, means avoiding the death penalty, not obtaining an acquittal. A winning strategy usually involves the jury knowing the accused and understanding why he committed the crime.

When we brainstormed McVeigh's defense at the Trial College, we felt the jury must understand the militia movement and its connections, directly or indirectly, to McVeigh. They must feel his hatred for government. They must know those behind the scenes who motivate far-right superpatriots to kill. They must see him as the pawn I believe he was.

Stephen Jones may have considered a similar defense strategy. In a press statement released the day McVeigh was indicted, Jones criticized the president's hasty decision to seek the death penalty without knowing "the range of social, political, economic and psychological forces that drove [the bomber] to commit an act so unthinkable to most." He concluded that "we can honor those who died" without sentencing the guilty party to death, if our desire for retribution is tempered with "a measure of compassion" for "someone who could harbor that kind of anger and hatred."

Assuming he is guilty, understanding McVeigh's motives could also help expose the threat posed by America's militia movement. Many believe McVeigh, if convicted, should be executed, but that aside, the following argument might be the only one that could save his life. It might also help expose the threat posed by America's militia movement.

Ladies and gentlemen of the jury, Timothy McVeigh bombed the Alfred P. Murrah Federal Building. He is responsible for the brutal deaths of 169 men, women, and children. You do not need to spend time deciding whether he committed this horrible crime.

There is no excuse, not even one, that rational, civilized people can accept to justify what he did. In fact, no rational, sane, civilized person would fill a truck with explosives, drive it in front of a public building, and end the lives of innocent little children playing in a nursery. You know this. The judge knows this. The nation knows this.

The law, though, in its infinite wisdom, does provide a defense for Timothy. Not an excuse, but a legal defense the court will tell you that you must consider. I only ask now, as you hear the evidence, that you allow for the possibility that Timothy believed he had no choice but to destroy that building to save his country. He struck a blow for freedom that, in his mind, he was compelled to do.


It would take at least a day to complete this opening statement. The jury would learn about McVeigh's obsession with his hero in *The Turner Diaries* who blew up a federal building; his valiant service in the Desert Storm campaign; his anguish at seeing American soldiers serving under United Nations command in Somalia; his fears that our country's values will be lost to a godless one-world government; his outrage that FBI agents would murder innocent women and children; his anger at corrupt, overpaid politicians.

These are apparently McVeigh's deeply felt beliefs. To him they are as real as the disgust I feel for the bombing. If guilty, I believe he probably honestly

believed he had to sound an alarm to wake up a sleeping people before we all become slaves to a tyrannical
government. Perhaps he sees himself as a brave warrior
destined to slay this evil dragon. He loves his country.
He is, he believes, a true patriot.

William Pierce, McVeigh's literary mentor, understood this type of patriotism. He told his radio audience
in the week after the bombing that many Americans
had "come to consider the U.S. government their worst
enemy." Just as McVeigh told his local New York community two years earlier that he felt pressure to correct
America's problems—"Do we have to shed blood to
reform the current system?"—so Pierce said, "There are
some who feel a sense of responsibility to do something
about that enemy."

McVeigh might say, if he's guilty, that he did not
want people to suffer. How could he wish pain and suffering upon small children when he wrote a letter to
his hometown newspaper—three years before the
bombing—condemning the cruel slaughter of cattle for
food?

> It is inhumane to line cattle up side by side with
> their heads and necks protruding over a low fence,
> and walk from one end to the other, slitting their
> throats with either a machete or a power saw. Unable
> to run or move, they are left there to bleed to death.

If McVeigh is guilty, he surely would have felt the
powerful explosion while driving away from Oklahoma
City, and probably would have turned to *The Turner
Diaries* to console his conscience: "There is no way we
can destroy the System without hurting innocent people. It is a heavy burden of responsibility for us to bear
since most of the victims of our bomb were only

pawns who were no more committed to the sick philosophy . . . of the System than we are."

Timothy McVeigh, if guilty, probably believed he
was a good soldier compelled to kill innocent people in
time of war for a higher goal.

He and those he admires in the militia movement
believe America is at war with its people. The higher
goal is saving our democracy. Perhaps this proud soldier has simply done his duty.

I do not think for a minute a jury would buy this
defense and find McVeigh not guilty by reason of insan-
ity, irresistible impulse, or compulsion. That was not
the goal of our Trial College defense strategy. It was to
set the stage for the penalty trial and to maybe save
McVeigh's life.

Jurors who hear a capital defendant put on a phony
defense are unlikely to be sympathetic when he later
begs for his life. If they can relate to him as a human
being, feel in some small personal way what might
have motivated him to act, his chance for mercy
improves. None of the jurors would bomb a building,
but it is highly likely that some would share his
antigovernment feelings. These jurors might see how
the hateful teachings of Louis Beam, Pete Peters, and
William Pierce may have pushed this ex-soldier off the
edge. McVeigh needs only a few jurors who can accept
that good men, men who fought for their country and
faced death on the battlefield, could become twisted by
hateful propaganda that might lead them to commit a
terrible crime.

In today's antigovernment climate, sympathetic
jurors might be more numerous than one might expect.
A man from California wrote me after my appearance
on *Larry King Live* that while he did not condone the
bombing, he had had enough frustrations with govern-

ment "to understand why some people resort to such actions."

It is only speculation to predict how a jury trying McVeigh and Nichols will react in the confines of a pan-eled federal courtroom over a year after the bombing. The Patriot movement and its leaders reacted quickly and predictably.

In a hotel ballroom in Branson, Missouri, the new capital of country music, there were "no tears for the mangled and dead of Oklahoma City, no prayers for lost babies and weeping mothers," noted our investigator Mike Reynolds.

But there was plenty of hate toward the govern-ment.

# Children for Children

As Mike Reynolds settled into his chair among the six hundred Christian Patriots gathered in the large Crystal Hall of the Lodge of the Ozarks Hotel in Branson, Missouri, Christian Identity Pastor Pete Peters took the stage.

Peters was not scheduled to speak that Friday, April 21, the first day of the conference. But he had some important news for the assembly that couldn't wait. He had been on the telephone with his people in Colorado, said Peters, and they told him the government had linked the Oklahoma bombing to white supremacists.

He then asked the audience to join him in prayer.

Three years earlier, Pastor Peters had led a similar audience at Estes Park, Colorado, in a prayer for the souls of Vicki and Samuel Weaver, who had been killed by federal lawmen at Ruby Ridge. But the prayer he offered in Branson was not for the souls of the 169 men, women, and children killed in the Oklahoma City bombing. It was for the 600 like-minded Christian Patriots who saw the bombing as a government-inspired plot to turn public opinion against the growing Patriot movement.

"Oh, Lord Yahweh, our creator, Yahshua, his son. Deliver us from the anti-Christ enemies who plot against us; strike them down! Thwart their satanic plot against your people! Keep us, your people Israel, safe from your enemy, the anti-Christs who have done this thing and put it on us, your people! We pray, in Christ's name. Amen."

Throughout the three-day conference in Branson there would be little sympathy shown for the Oklahoma City victims.

The callous attitude toward the bombing was best summed up by a broad-faced Oklahoma farmer Mike had shared a sink with in the bathroom. "They've been taking this country from us piece by piece for years," the man said as he stared directly at Mike, "but we got a piece of it back in Oklahoma City."

Mike recalled the photograph of a blood-streaked baby held by a fireman that appeared on the front page of nearly every daily newspaper in America. He fought back his anger at this so-called Christian Patriot, excused himself, and returned to the hall to complete his intelligence assignment.

The Second Annual Super Conference of the International Coalition of Covenant Congregations was Mike's second stop on his intelligence-gathering trip for the Militia Task Force of our Klanwatch Project.

His first stop, an event on April 19 to commemorate Waco and to protest Snell's execution, had ended before it had started. Heavy rains, a strong police and media presence, and the explosion at the Oklahoma City federal building earlier that morning kept people away from the Confederate memorial park in western Arkansas.

Mike chose the Branson meeting because it was an Identity-sponsored event timed near April 19 that counted among its attendees many of the Estes Park crowd, including Peters and militia proponent Larry Pratt.

While flags were flying at half-staff all over the nation and ministers were offering prayers for the suffering, Pratt, the director of Gun Owners of America, continued his promotion of private armies.

"We have a lot of confusion in our land and the bottom line is that it is a spiritual battle," Pratt told the hushed audience. "This is not a political issue. What I see in Scripture is not that we have a right to keep and bear arms, but that we have a responsibility to do so."

Earl Jones of the Christian Crusade for Truth out of New Mexico and a close confidant of Louis Beam told the audience it was necessary to retake America for God's chosen people. Mike put his pen down. He was all too familiar with Jones's strategy.

The ramrod straight, former ex–Marine colonel had already urged many in the group to adopt Louis Beam's leaderless resistance concept of small cells answerable to no one. He had told them at Estes Park that the strategy left men "free to do everything on their own, just as one man or several . . . whatever comes into their hearts to do."

Speaker after speaker tried to turn attention away from the tragedy in Oklahoma City and back to the deaths at Waco.

"People don't talk about that tragedy," David Barley of America's Promise Ministry in Idaho told the group. "They don't talk about the little children they murdered. They show pictures of these precious little children— and they were precious little children—who died in this accident. I don't see any pictures of what happened in Waco.

"The media asks who are these evil cowards who were the perpetrators of this bomb?" Barley said. "Well, I have another question. Who were the evil cowards who hid themselves and murdered those little children in Waco, Texas?"

W. N. Otwell, a fiery pastor who runs a well-armed compound in east Texas, had little sympathy for the women and children killed in Oklahoma City. He told the group it was God's retribution for the deaths at Waco. "You look at the Old Testament," he shouted. "God did not mind killing a bunch of women and kids. God talks about slaughter. Don't leave one suckling. Don't leave no babies. Don't leave nothing. Kill them! Destroy them."

With God's admonition and blessing, the battle was now joined. The new cry from Peters, Beam, William Pierce, and a thousand militia leaders would revive Waco. The militia organizers had been handed a perfect mirror comparison, blood for blood, children for children.

It was a mirror militia members held up to the rest of the nation.

"Blaming the bombing in Oklahoma City on the militia, or unnamed 'patriots,' is an obscenity," Louis Beam wrote in the 1995 May/June issue of *The Jubilee*. "For it was, after all, the taking of lives by the government at Ruby Ridge and Waco that provided the innocent blood that gave birth to the militia and the associated anti-government feeling currently sweeping the nation."

The Militia of Montana issued a press release that reminded followers that "the innocent at Mount Carmel"—the site of the Branch Davidian compound outside of Waco—cried out for justice just as much as the "hearts of the innocent in Oklahoma City."

Beam, the Trochmanns, and other militia leaders combined the supposed moral equivalency of Oklahoma and Waco with a second line of thought that laid the blame for the bombing at the government's feet.

"Those who know and study history can reasonably assume the government was behind the Oklahoma City bombing," said Beam.

Why, he asked, did the government need a bombing with such loss of life? It was, he answered, to build public pressure for passage of the Comprehensive Terrorism Prevention Act of 1995, a measure designed to stop the growing militia movement. Another reason: "A dam of dead bodies to hold back the flood of opposition" to Washington's corruption, racketeering, and abuse of human rights.

The Trochmanns claimed they had evidence that two explosions occurred and that the bombs used were prototypes being built by the federal government.

"Something definitely smells bad here. It smells purely military."

The theme that the government was somehow involved with the bombing reverberated throughout the movement.

"I mean, who's got a track record of killing children?" asked Indiana militia leader Linda Thompson, who then pointed to Ruby Ridge and Waco for the answer.

Beam called on the "unsung heroes" in the movement to rise in opposition to the state tyranny that he predicted would come from the bombing, as federal agents are "ordered to enforce totalitarian rule."

"The liberty bell has begun to ring loudly," he proclaimed to the thousands of militia members and racist fanatics who see his words as gospel, "and would-be federal tyrants know for whom the bell tolls."

Still a third line of thought that ran through the Patriot movement, often in conjunction with one or both of the others, was proffered by William Pierce. The Oklahoma City bombing, he said, was the opening shot of a new revolution. Domestic terrorism was an inevitable response to a murderous criminal government, he argued.

Pierce delivered a carefully crafted speech a week after the bombing on his radio show, *American Dissident Voices*. It was designed in part to firm up the backbone of the movement's newest members, those who weren't, as yet, fully immersed in the movement's ideological beliefs. He wanted them to know what would be expected of them following the bombing and why.

Pierce began as if speaking from the Oval Office, addressing the country after a national tragedy.

> Hello, my fellow Americans and all my friends around the world.
>
> When a government engages in terrorism against its own citizens, it should not be surprised when some of those citizens strike back and engage in terrorism against the government.
>
> Terrorism is nasty business . . . but terrorism is a form of warfare and, in war, most of the victims are noncombatants.
>
> Certainly none of us condone the killing of children. But in fact, it is the Clinton government which has led the way in killing of children. The hatred one hears in [Clinton's and Reno's] voices when they talk about the Oklahoma City bombers is not because children were killed, it's because they know the bombing was aimed at them.
>
> Americans haven't had a real war fought on their own sod for 130 years. . . . I think things are about to change.

## MARTYRS OF THE MODERN MILITIA MOVEMENT

Gordon Kahl, Posse Comitatus leader, died in a shootout with federal agents at his Arkansas hideout in 1983. He led a tax protest movement during the 1980s farm crisis. (Police arrest photo)

Robert Mathews died on Whidbey Island, Washington, in 1984 in a house fire during an FBI siege. He founded the neo-Nazi group The Order. (Bettmann Archive)

Richard Wayne Snell, a Christian Identity leader, was executed in Arkansas on April 19, 1995. He killed a black state trooper and a pawnshop owner he thought was Jewish. (*Arkansas Democrat-Gazette*)

Alan Berg, a Jewish radio talk show host who denounced right-wing groups, was gunned down in his Denver driveway in June 1984 by Order members at the direction of Robert Mathews. FBI arrests halted a series of planned assassinations. I was at the top of Mathews's hit list but was saved by a warning from an FBI informant. (Lyn Alweis/*Denver Post*)

*Above:* Louis Beam was arrested in Waco, Texas, for criminal trespass at FBI's Branch Davidian news conference on March 18, 1993. The charges were later dismissed. (AP/Wide World Photos)

*Left:* Louis Beam rallying Klansmen to drive Vietnamese fishermen from Galveston Bay in 1981. (Klanwatch)

Members of Louis Beam's 2,500-man Texas Emergency Reserve paramilitary army terrorized Vietnamese fishermen in 1981 by riding "gun boat" near the docks and fishing fleets of the immigrants. Our lawsuit forced Beam to disband his paramilitary army. (John R. Van Beekum)

Glenn Miller, a former Green Beret and Order member, shouts commands to his White Patriot Party paramilitary unit in 1985 during a North Carolina street march. Miller's 1,000-man unit, trained in secret camps, plotted to blow up a federal power dam. Richard Cohen and I acted as special federal prosecutors and helped convict Miller of using stolen military weapons to operate an illegal private army. (Klanwatch)

Roger Handley and Terry Tucker, in uniform, at a secret Klan Special Forces paramilitary camp hidden in the north Alabama mountains. Both were convicted in 1989 for using militia units to harass blacks. We brought a suit that enjoined operation of the Klan Special Forces. (Christopher Bell, Decatur, Ala.)

Randy Weaver and his family in 1989, the year FBI agents recorded him selling a sawed-off shotgun to an undercover agent. Son Samuel and wife Vicki were killed by FBI sharpshooters at the cabin during the August 1992 standoff. (Weaver family photo)

The Weavers' cabin atop Ruby Ridge in Boundary County, Idaho, was built by Randy and Vicki in 1984 to escape modern civilization. Federal agents conducted surveillance of the cabin with hidden video cameras for months. (*Spokesman-Review*/Shawn Jacobson)

Over one hundred protesters gathered at the roadblock leading to the Weavers' cabin during the eleven-day siege in August 1992. The angry group, including neighbors, skinheads, and a mix of far-right patriots, shouted insults at federal agents. (*Spokesman-Review*/Jesse Tinsley)

The federal government assembled a small military base about a mile from the Weavers' cabin after the shoot-out began. Over three hundred federal and state agents participated in the arrest attempt. (*Spokesman-Review*/Colin Mulvany)

*Right:* Retired Green Beret Lt. Col. James "Bo" Gritz carried a letter to Randy Weaver from Christian Identity minister Pete Peters urging him to give up. Gritz negotiated Weaver's surrender. He talks with reporters at a roadblock in August 1992. (*Spokesman-Review*/Anne C. Williams)

*Below:* Federal agents search the ashes of the Branch Davidian compound in April 1993, finding over 191 rifles, plus machine guns and grenade launchers. Four ATF agents and eighty-one Davidians died during the fifty-one-day siege. Waco equaled Ruby Ridge as an organizing issue for the militia and Patriot movements. (John Mantel/Sipa)

Christian Identity minister Pete Peters organized the October 1992 Estes Park, Colorado, meeting in reaction to the Weaver killings. The 160 attendees included Louis Beam and a wide spectrum of far-right leaders. (*Ft. Collins Colorodoan*)

Larry Pratt, founder of the Virginia-based Gun Owners of America, lent mainstream respectability to the Estes Park gathering. He urged the formation of armed militias. He resigned as co-chairman of Patrick Buchanan's 1996 presidential campaign after his militia connections were exposed. (Jennifer Warburg)

Shortly after the Weaver siege and the Estes Park meeting in late 1992, large quantities of citizen militia–organizing manuals began appearing at gun shows across the nation, like this one held at the Springdale, Arkansas, Holiday Inn, on July 1, 1995. (Tom Ewart)

The Alfred P. Murrah Federal Building in Oklahoma City shortly after the April 19, 1995, explosion that killed 169 people. A similar explosion is described in *The Turner Diaries*, a fictional account of a race war led by an underground citizen militia group to purge the nation of nonwhites and Jews. (AP/Wide World Photos)

Timothy McVeigh in federal custody in Perry, Oklahoma. He was an ardent disciple of *The Turner Diaries* and sold copies at gun shows. He attended Michigan Militia meetings. (AP/Wide World Photos)

Terry Nichols, in custody after being charged in the bombing, was McVeigh's army buddy. Nichols allegedly helped McVeigh purchase and store the nitrogen fertilizer used in the Oklahoma City bombing. (AP/Wide World Photos)

William Pierce, the real author of *The Turner Diaries*, operates the National Alliance, a secretive neo-Nazi group. He warns his followers that they should be prepared to kill to save the white race. (F. Brian Ferguson)

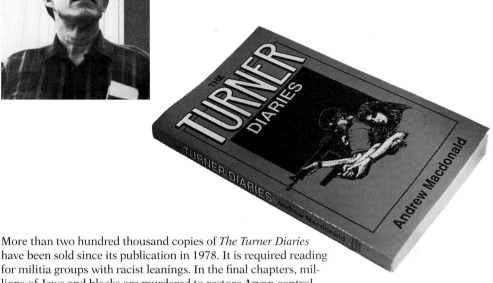

More than two hundred thousand copies of *The Turner Diaries* have been sold since its publication in 1978. It is required reading for militia groups with racist leanings. In the final chapters, millions of Jews and blacks are murdered to restore Aryan control.

John Trochmann, founder of the Militia of Montana, holding the group's 1995 mail-order catalog, which offers videotapes and books on militia organizing and training. Trochmann, a frequent visitor to the neo-Nazi Aryan Nations compound, has helped organize dozens of militia units across the country. (*Spokesman-Review*/Dan McComb)

Col. Dennis Mizisin of the Central Michigan Regional Militia swears in Richard Sovis to the rank of captain in November 1994. The unit is one of forty-nine militias in the state. (Doug Elliard/*Flint Journal*)

Michigan Militia cofounder Norman Olson, a Baptist minister, in his Dexter, Michigan, gun store. He claims ten thousand militia members in 1995. He denies being racist, but blamed the Japanese for plotting to bomb the Oklahoma City federal building. (Paul Paiewonsky/Matrix)

Members of the Gadsden, Alabama, Minutemen practice firearms exercises. Mark Koernke of the Michigan Militia helped form this deep-South militia unit. The group claimed several thousand members in 1995. (Joe Songer/*Birmingham News*)

A unit of the Michigan Militia, May 1995. Members range from bricklayers to lawyers. Most have no racist ties, but all fear the federal government. They train to defend against federal oppression and a takeover by a one-world government. (Nina Berman)

*Right:* Weapons seized by the Fowlerville, Michigan, police in a routine traffic stop in March 1995 from three members of a secret Michigan Militia cell. A note in the car indicated the group was surveilling the police and intended to "neutralize" all targets identified. (Scott Piper/*Livingston County Press*)

*Below:* Army of Israel militiamen examine the close grouping of shots in the chest of a target, March 1995. The secretive unit trains near Hurricane, Utah. The group, not Jewish, takes its name from Christian Identity teachings that Aryans are the true lost tribe of Israel, God's chosen people. (Militia Task Force)

Member of a secret militia cell doing ambush training in north Idaho woods, November 1995. Militia of Montana sells paramilitary handbooks such as *Sniper Training and Employment, Guerrilla Warfare, Booby Traps,* and *Unconventional Warfare Devices and Techniques.* (*Spokesman-Review*/Dan McComb)

Secret militia cell on military exercises in an area not far from Randy Weaver's Ruby Ridge, Idaho, cabin, November 1995. The unit specializes in long-range sniper shots. A wealthy businessman helps finance the cell. (*Spokesman-Review*/Dan McComb)

John Trochmann (*left*) testified with militia leaders before the Senate Judiciary Committee's Subcommittee on Terrorism, Technology and Government Information on July 15, 1995. He said the militia movement was a giant neighborhood watch, standing up to governmental oppression and tyranny. (AP/Wide World Photos)

A member of the Gadsden, Alabama, Minutemen militia group instructs a ten-year-old boy in marksmanship, June 1995. A Wisconsin militia leader urged arming youths: "I want you to do the most loving thing . . . buy each of your children an SKS [assault] rifle and five hundred rounds of ammunition." (AP/Wide World Photos)

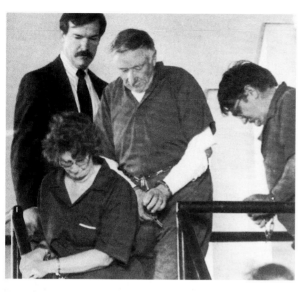

*Left:* Willie Ray Lampley and these members of his Oklahoma Constitutional Militia were arrested by the FBI on November 13, 1995, in a plot to bomb the Southern Poverty Law Center. The FBI claimed that they were building a fertilizer bomb like the one allegedly used in Oklahoma City by Timothy McVeigh. (AP/Wide World Photos)

*Below:* Militia and key racist groups target civil rights organizations and government agencies in concerted intelligence-gathering efforts using SALUTE forms (an acronym for the data sought). This operation was discovered by the Militia Task Force in August 1995.

AIYAN

NATIONS

CLASSIFICATION
GENERAL ST

SECURITY/INT
POLITICAL I

STANDARD F

TO:

FROM:

ROUTE T

DATE:

ACTION REQUEST:

SALUTE REPORT

S-SIZE-What was the size of the en

A-ACTIVITY-What was the enemy do

L-LOCATION Exactly where was the

U-UNIT- What enemy organization
Anti Klan Committee etc.

T-TIME- When was the enemy gro

E-EQUIPMENT- What equipment
Anti Racist but we're able

Access enemy intent PERCEPT

OTHER GENERAL OBSERVATIONS

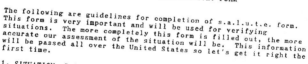

**Tri-State Militia**
*2nd Brigade*
# 4th Division
Light Mechanized Cavalry
*"Ground Mobile"*

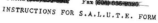

P.O. Box 355
Gregory, SD 57533
Phone (605) 835-5046    Fax (605) 835-8396

### INSTRUCTIONS FOR S.A.L.U.T.E. FORM

The following are guidelines for completion of s.a.l.u.t.e. form. This form is very important and will be used for verifying situations. The more completely this form is filled out, the more accurate our assessment of the situation will be. This information will be passed all over the United States so let's get it right the first time.

1. SITUATION: Brief: Give an overview of the situation and reported status of crisis. Classification will be determined by C.I.C. Commander.

2. SIZE: Brief: This deals with actual number of people involved in the situation. This includes good guys, bad guys, troops, etc...

3. ACTIVITY: Brief: This deals with what the people involved (good guys, bad guys, troops, etc...) are doing at the present time.

4. LOCATION: Brief: THIS IS VERY IMPORTANT. This deals with pinpointing the location of the reported situation, i.e. state, city, county, direction of movement, highways, mile markers etc...

5. UNIT: Brief: This deals with the various kinds of good guys and/or bad guys reportedly involved. If Military get specific unit designations such as shoulder patches etc...

6. TIME: Brief: This is the time and date the incident occurred and list specific time zone. NOT THE TIME SITUATION WAS CALLED IN TO C.I.C. Use Military Time on all C.I.C. Reports.

7. EQUIPMENT: Brief: If aircraft used get type, number, and markings. If ground equipment used get type, number, and bumper markings. Note: We can tell a lot from bumper markings. If rail designation direction and which rail line.

Logged In: Name of personnel taking report.
Time: Time report was taken.
Date: Date report was taken.

ALL REPORTS ARE TO BE TURNED IN TO C.I.C. COMMAND ONCE COMPLETED.

Major Parsons, C.I.C. Commander

Chuck Harder broadcasts daily on over three hundred mainly small-town radio stations from his White Springs, Florida, studio. He is the king of grassroots airways. His message: The government defrauds, lies to, and rapes the people. He is joined in this message by Rush Limbaugh, G. Gordon Liddy, and dozens of government bashers on over one thousand stations. (Tara McParland/*Florida Times-Union*)

Groups like the Taxpayers United for Fairness of Sandpoint, Idaho, are not racists or bomb throwers. They pledge the flag with pride, but do not fully trust the government. They do not understand why federal agents killed Randy Weaver's son and wife. Some watch militia videos, unaware that mean-spirited racists want them as foot soldiers. (*Spokesman-Review*/Dan McComb)

"I suspect Americans will begin engaging in terrorism on a scale the world has never known," Pierce said, using the same not-so-subtle-suggestions to engage in violence that perhaps McVeigh followed from Pierce's *Turner Diaries*.

Pierce also provided the targets. Jewish media bosses and commentators with their snouts in the media trough. Homosexuals, career women, and minorities enjoying special privileges gained through artificial equality. Nonwhites from the Third World and illegal immigrants from Mexico. Politicians who vote oppressive taxes and restrictive rules and regulations. ATF and FBI baby killers. Young whites singing rap diddies and behaving like blacks.

He claims one hundred thousand hear his radio broadcast.

"When people are pushed as far as they are willing to go and when they believe they have nothing to lose," he said, "then they will resort to terrorism. There will be more and more such people in the future."

William Pierce, I believe, sees the Oklahoma City bombing as the type of ad hoc terrorism that will ultimately restore white Aryans to power. It was important for him to have his followers see the bombing in perspective.

"We should help the more perceptive members of the public to see terrorism in its context, rather than as a series of individual acts." This context, he said, is private terrorism responding to government terrorism. "The more repressive and terroristic the government becomes, the more individuals there will be who will engage in terrorism to get back at the government."

He predicted the violence would get worse. "There is nothing the government can do to stop it," he concluded. "The bond of trust between the U.S. government and its citizens has been broken. It's far too late to mend it."

The horror of the tragedy in Oklahoma City threatened the militia movement's access to the larger, more mainstream segment of the "weapons culture" that Pierce and others had been cultivating. The less ideological among that group began to wonder if ballots weren't preferable to bullets. Some left immediately after the bombing. Others would be scared away in the months to come.

By making Waco the moral equivalent of Oklahoma City, Pierce, Beam, and other leaders in the militia and Patriot movement hoped to steady their newly recruited foot soldiers and keep them shoulder-to-shoulder with the true believers.

# Bonds of Trust

Almost ten thousand people packed the State Fairgrounds Arena in Oklahoma City, mourning the dead and struggling to understand the tragedy. Thousands more stood outside in the raw wind or watched the memorial service on a big screen at a nearby ballpark.

Unlike the Christian Identity meeting being held in Branson's Crystal Hall that same Sunday, the speakers did not call for purchasing assault rifles or for joining militias. They did not give holy justification for a bloody cleansing of anti-Christ enemies. They did not condemn the government.

The service at the Oklahoma fairgrounds arena opened with "Amazing Grace." Some mourners sang; others silently wept. The nation watched as Reverend Billy Graham tried to provide solace, comfort, and hope. Strangers, standing in line at the arena, cried in the arms of other strangers. Cathy Keating, wife of Oklahoma governor Frank Keating, told the hushed, somber gathering, "Our wounds are deep and our scars are raw."

America's most deadly domestic terrorist attack touched everyone, except maybe hardened soldiers of the Patriot movement who were convinced, like William Pierce, that "there is no way we can destroy the System without hurting many thousands of innocent people."

No one at the ceremony mentioned the Branch Davidian compound near Waco or Randy Weaver's cabin on Ruby Ridge. That would come later. The focus of the nation's outrage demanded immediate attention from the highest levels of government.

President Clinton stood in the arena where rodeo cowboys wrestle steers and ride angry bulls and asked for God's strength and healing. Our country must purge itself, he said, "of the dark forces that give rise to this evil."

"The bombing in Oklahoma City was an attack on innocent children and defenseless citizens," Clinton had told the country the day after the tragedy. "The United States will not tolerate it, and I will not allow the people of this country to be intimidated by evil cowards."

He promised a massive federal response. "Let there be no room for doubt. We will find the people who did this," he promised. "When we do, justice will be swift, certain, and severe."

Clinton drew a bead on the Patriot movement, the militias, and the growing antigovernment culture in a speech at Michigan State University a few days later. "There is nothing patriotic about hating your government, or pretending you can hate government and love your country. How dare you suggest that we in the freest nation on earth live in tyranny," he exclaimed. "How dare you call yourselves patriots and heroes."

His first target was the bombers. "If this is not a crime for which capital punishment is called," he told the thirty-five thousand students, "I don't know what is."

His next target was domestic groups that advocate and use violence for political or religious goals. "I don't think we have to give up our liberties," he said, sensitive to heavy-handed FBI tactics used to investigate civil rights and antiwar activists in the 1960s and 1970s. But, he said, "We have to have more discipline and we have to be willing to see serious threats to our lives and property investigated."

FBI guidelines at the time of the bombing were interpreted to forbid investigation of domestic groups unless there was a "reasonable indication" that they were trying to achieve their goals through violence or some other form of action that would violate federal criminal laws. "That meant," a retired former senior FBI official told the *New York Times*, "you have to wait until you have blood in the streets before the Bureau can act. You can't prevent what you don't know about and you can't know about a group if you can't investigate until after they have committed an act of terrorism."

President Clinton hoped his proposals to Congress would give federal agents more freedom to gather needed information on domestic terrorists. The Omnibus Counter-Terrorism Act of 1995 had been introduced at his request in February in response to the World Trade Center bombing. It dealt only with foreign terrorism. His new proposals would drastically alter the way domestic groups could be tracked.

Clinton's proposals were delivered to the Senate Judiciary Committee eight days after the bombing by FBI Director Louis Freeh and Deputy Attorney General Jamie Gorelick. It was the opening day of hearings titled "Terrorism in the United States: The Nature and Extent of the Threat and Possible Legislative Responses." I was also invited to testify.

Ms. Gorelick told the senators that the challenge was to "prove that we have the will and power to fulfill a fundamental responsibility set out in the first sentence of our Constitution, to 'insure domestic tranquillity.'" To ensure that the terrorists do not win, she said, law enforcement needed adequate tools.

These needed tools included one thousand new agents, prosecutors, and support personnel, estimated to cost $1.25 billion over five years; the creation of an interagency Domestic Counter-Terrorism Center headed by the FBI to collect, analyze, and disseminate information; easy access to credit records without court authorization; the ability to track suspected terrorists' telephone traffic with "pen registers" and "trap and trace" devices; the same free access to records from hotels, motels, and common carriers for domestic counterterrorism as in national security matters; funding of the "digital telephone bill" to assure court-authorized access to digitized communications; military participation in crime fighting when weapons of mass destruction are involved; and the availability of electronic surveillance and roving wiretaps when it is not possible to specify telephone numbers to be tapped.

Another administration proposal was to require the inclusion of "taggants"—microscopic particles—in standard raw materials used in explosive devices to permit tracing of the materials after an explosion.

FBI Director Freeh told the committee that there were individuals and groups arming themselves to further social and political goals. One of their goals, he said, might be "to murder as many people as possible through a single blow." He assured the senators that the FBI had no concern with a group "simply because of its ideology or political philosophy" but "cannot and should not, however, tolerate and ignore individuals or groups who advocate violence." If Congress and the people wanted the FBI to assume broader powers, he promised to carry them out. He did acknowledge that under existing guidelines, more investigations could be initiated.

Freeh told the senators that domestic terrorists who "would kill innocent Americans . . . American kids . . . are not just enemies of the United States, they are enemies of mankind."

Civil liberties groups voiced concern, as did some senators, that giving federal law enforcement agencies these broad new powers to investigate domestic groups would curtail constitutional rights. They cautioned against hasty overreaction.

President Clinton said some inconvenience must be tolerated for public safety. He pointed out that while people complained at first about metal detectors in airports, they now accepted them.

I gave the Senate committee members our assessment of the threat posed by paramilitary groups, especially those influenced by racists. We had identified, by that time, almost 150 militia groups operating in thirty-three states. At least thirty-six had ties to the white supremacist movement. Our experience with paramilitary organizations in Texas and North Carolina had convinced us, I explained, that when militia members grew "bored with roaming the woods and shooting at paper targets," they would turn their sights on innocent people. To curb the threat, I recommended that the committee consider a federal law that would regulate militia groups that were not authorized by state law.

I told the committee that I opposed a major overhaul of the Attorney General's Guidelines Concerning Domestic Security/Terrorist Investigations, except to allow the collection of publicly available information. It would not violate the First Amendment for the Justice Department, I suggested, to maintain, for example, newspaper clippings of calls to violence even if the rhetoric did not amount to incitement and was couched in terms of "self-defense." Without the ability to gather this kind of information, federal officials could easily miss a piece of a puzzle that would, in the words of the Guidelines, "reasonably indicate that two or more persons are engaged in an enterprise for the purpose of furthering political or social goals wholly or in part through activities that involve force or violence and a violation of the criminal laws of the United States."

By gathering this type of information, our Klanwatch staff in 1986 had been alerted to plans by Glenn Miller and his North Carolina White Patriot Party to wreak havoc with stolen military explosives. We provided this information to the Justice Department. They were reluctant to monitor the group because of a restrictive reading of the Guidelines. It was not until we almost had "blood-in-the-street" evidence that Justice got involved. Even then, it took a criminal contempt of court proceeding with Richard Cohen, my law partner, and me acting as specially appointed federal prosecutors to end Miller's illegal activity and put his militia group out of business.

Clinton's proposed legislation passed the Senate quickly by the lopsided vote of 91 to 8. Two weeks later, a similar measure was approved by the House Judiciary Committee by a vote of 23 to 12.

Despite the horror of the Oklahoma City tragedy and the momentum to respond legislatively, the Clinton administration's proposals stalled. Senate hearings, one on the Waco siege and another on the Weaver shootings, wrangling over amendments to the antiterrorism bill, and an unlikely coalition of special-interest groups would doom Clinton's antiterrorism bill, at least for 1995.

During the first few weeks after the tragedy, many militia leaders condemned the bombing. "There is no justification for brutality meeting brutality," Norman Olson, commander of the Michigan Militia, told the *Washington Post*. Joseph Nee, a Colorado militia leader, called those responsible "scumbags."

Ted Koppel broadcast *Nightline* a week after the bombing from the United Methodist Church in James Nichols's farming community of Decker, Michigan. Art Bean, commander of the Tuscola County Militia Brigade, told Koppel, "We are Americans. We believe in free speech. We believe in the Constitution, and we believe in the rights of other people." Ray Southwell, cofounder of the Michigan Militia, said, "We're fearful of our government. We're fearful of terrorism going on [against] the American people. Our sheriffs are our first line of defense." Norman Olson told Americans that he wanted the government to "give the power back to the people."

The militia was there to protect the public in case government agents attack, uniformed members told Koppel. They were not violent. They had no plans to start a revolution. They were just politically concerned citizens forming militias like their forefathers had done when the colonies faced a tyrannical King George. This message was repeated by clean-shaven, business-attired, middle-aged militia members for television cameras, *Newsweek*, *Time*, and dozens of newspapers.

I was on a lot of those same television shows, not opposite militia members, but giving our take on what the militias were really up to. I explained I knew of no country except America that tolerated private armies that could train with assault weapons and learn how to build bombs. Although about half the states had laws strictly forbidding militias and many more had made certain types of paramilitary training illegal, the laws were almost never enforced. Many who heard me had already bought into the user-friendly image militia leaders were peddling. Some let me know they saw the groups as harmless, only exercising the right to assemble peacefully.

"I am not now, nor have I ever been a member of a militia group," a man wrote me, "but I can surely understand why citizens would band together for their own defense." Another wrote, "The militia spokesmen I have heard on television say their purpose is to make government stay within the bounds of the constitution. I see nothing wrong with that."

In response to negative publicity about militias following the Oklahoma City bombing, militia leaders like Norman Olson and Ray Southwell began making bold allegations of government complicity in the bombings. In a press release dated May 4, 1995, the two said the bombing was masterminded by Japanese officials with the assistance of the U.S. government. This absurd statement resulted in their forced resignation as commanders of the Michigan Militia. They later regrouped as the Northern Michigan Regional Militia. Olson said his old group had been overrun by moderates.

Some in Congress were not so sure how moderate the militia movement really was. They wanted to expose violence-prone leaders like Louis Beam. Prior to the bombing, Senator Arlen Specter had scheduled hearings on the Waco and Weaver incidents. Representative Charles Schumer, a Democrat of New York, also wanted in-depth hearings on the militias. Speaker Newt

Gingrich refused. Specter, a Republican and then a candidate for his party's presidential nomination, wanted the spotlight focused on what went wrong at Waco and Ruby Ridge.

Senator Specter finally agreed to one-day militia hearings before his Subcommittee on Terrorism, Technology and Government Information. He invited Militia of Montana's John Trochmann, Ken Adams, and Robert Fletcher; former Michigan Militia leaders Norman Olson and Ray Southwell; and Ohio militia leader James Johnson. A panel of law enforcement officers testified that the militias were the aggressors, "disturbing and dangerous."

The militia leaders appeared anything but dangerous. Disturbed, maybe, because of their wild claims, but not dangerous. Norman Olson repeated his group's charges that the U.S. government manipulated the weather, causing tornadoes to disorient heartland America, and had assisted in the nerve gas attacks on the Tokyo subway. All the claims had been documented, he explained. He promised to provide the proof.

Senator Specter played into this ridiculous spectacle. He tried to pin Olson down on statements allegedly made to reporters that he could "understand" why someone would bomb the Oklahoma federal building.

Bristling with anger, Olson said, "You're trying to make us out to be something we're not. . . . We stand against corruption and tyranny. . . . There is intelligent life west of the Alleghenies. . . . You're wasting precious time."

Robert Fletcher, John Trochmann's public relations specialist, raised doubt about the "intelligent life" claim. He testified that Attorney General Reno had hired 2,500 hit men and that secret United Nations military maneuvers were being conducted in our nation.

James Johnson, the only black on the panel and one of the few blacks I have heard about in the militias, testified that the animosity between the people and the government was frightening, that Americans were heavily armed, and that the militias were "the ones who calm people down."

Phil Donahue was better prepared to question some of the same militia members who appeared on his show in late 1994 than this committee with its high-paid investigative staff and subpoena power. Specter should have asked Johnson how the militia calmed people down by providing members with books on how to use explosives. A few selected videos and military-type manuals from Trochmann's mail-order catalogue would have educated C-Span watchers and still possibly made the nightly news.

But the only hard question, or more correctly "accusation," was directed at the senators by Trochmann. "We stand against corruption and the tyranny of government," bald and bearded Trochmann angrily shouted at Senator Specter. "We're coming to believe you all stand for that corruption."

Specter, not used to invited panelists impugning his integrity, shot back like a pride-wounded schoolboy, "I don't take that lightly, your comment to me that I represent congressional corruption. I don't take that lightly at all. And I want you to prove it if you are going to say that."

This committee never indicated whether these private soldiers supplied proof of corruption or the documents Olson claimed "unnamed U.S. operatives" gave him proving collusion between our government and Japan in the Oklahoma bombing.

Most Americans watching the hearings might disagree with Ken Adams, who told the committee that the militias are a "cross-section of Americans, attorneys to doctors to mechanics . . . law abiding and God-fearing." But few watching the spectacle would see them as dangerous.

Representative Schumer, unable to hold his own official hearings, called the event "a soapbox for the radical right."

The hearings Specter held on Waco and Ruby Ridge would be quite different.

The bombing in Oklahoma occurred on the second anniversary of the fire that killed seventy-five people at the Branch Davidian compound. The same day the public watched pictures of cars burning outside the Alfred P. Murrah Federal Building, members of the Northeast Texas Militia erected a memorial at the burned-out Davidian compound. But more people than the militias were pointing to the Waco tragedy as a factor in the Oklahoma bombing.

No one was more sensitive to the comparison of the events than Attorney General Reno. She had given the final approval of the ill-fated FBI plan to rescue the children at Waco.

In remarks prepared for a ceremony to honor slain law enforcement officers in Newark, New Jersey, held less than a week after the Oklahoma bombing, Reno went on the defensive. "How could some people imply a moral equivalency between the government's efforts to save lives at Waco and the cruel indifferent taking of lives in Oklahoma?" Reno asked. David Koresh had "set a standard no civilized society can tolerate," she said. He accumulated weapons, ordered members to fire at federal agents, and had sexual relations with young girls. The anger over the deaths at Waco, Reno insisted, should be directed at Koresh, not federal agents.

Senator Specter opened his Waco hearings on June 15, 1995. The key issue, he said, was whether the government had been candid about the episode.

The Reverend Pete Peters and his Christian Identity brethren had grappled with how to embrace Waco without embracing the sinful lifestyle of David Koresh. They resolved the matter, seeing the government's murder of innocent people as the greater transgression. The same problem would also plague Specter.

One of the first witnesses on the opening day was Kiri Jewell.

Fourteen-year-old Kiri tearfully gave graphic testimony about how she was repeatedly sexually abused by Koresh. She was the Democrats' best witness, a favor allowed but later regretted by Republicans. Her testimony was powerful, taking a lot of steam out of Specter's planned assault on the ATF. The best evidence Specter offered of government misconduct was proof that the ATF had lost the element of surprise, yet proceeded with the raid. The FBI presented proof that Koresh's people, not the tank-led tear gas raid, caused the fire.

The FBI was the main target of Senator Specter's Weaver hearings in September.

Weaver was no saint, but this loyal family man had no criminal record before being arrested on a charge of selling two sawed-off shotguns to an ATF undercover informant. He had not raped young girls.

A little more than a year before the Weaver hearings began, an Idaho jury had found Kevin Harris and Randy Weaver not guilty of murdering U.S. Deputy

Marshal William Degan. Weaver had also been found not guilty of selling illegal shotguns.

Gerry Spence, the famed Wyoming trial lawyer, led a team of attorneys, including his son, Kent, in shattering the government's case. He provided Specter with a smoking gun. Spence proved that the FBI had created new rules of engagement for the Weaver siege. The FBI Hostage Rescue Team, flown in to "rescue" Weaver, his wife, and four children, was given permission to shoot to kill any armed male sighted outside the Weaver cabin, even if the person had not been given a chance to surrender. The normal rules provided that deadly force could only be used to prevent an imminent threat of serious harm to an agent or another person.

Spence can get to the essence of a case quicker than any lawyer I know. The defense to selling the sawed-off shotguns was entrapment; Marshal William Degan, Spence said, had been killed in self-defense. The real defense, Spence's trial theme, was that federal agents targeted Weaver for his unpopular beliefs and his ties to the neo-Nazi group Aryan Nations. To Spence, the issue was simple political persecution based on Weaver's religion and politics.

The ATF had known that Weaver frequented the Aryan Nations compound near his cabin long before taping him selling illegal shotguns to an informant. Spence contended that Weaver was set up because of his association with the group. After arresting Weaver, they offered him a deal. The charges would be dropped if he would spy for the ATF on Reverend Richard Butler and his Aryan Nations group. Weaver refused.

Spence convinced the jury that the government's intense interest in Weaver, the time and money spent watching his cabin before the shoot-out, and the new shoot-to-kill order were more appropriate for a Mafia operation than a small-time illegal gun trader.

The FBI initially withheld critical documents from the defense, especially those dealing with the new rules of engagement. The informant who purchased the guns from Weaver admitted on cross-examination that he did not expect to be paid by the ATF unless there was a conviction. Little went right for the prosecution. Weaver was convicted only for failing to appear for the trial on illegal gun sales charges and for committing crimes while on pretrial release. Weaver had already served fourteen of the eighteen-month sentence he received. Harris was acquitted of murdering the marshal and all related charges.

When Randy Weaver had agreed to surrender, he was promised a good lawyer. He got a great one who did not even charge for his services. I admire Gerry for making the justice system work for people like Randy Weaver.

The FBI's troubles did not end with the Weaver verdicts.

An early FBI internal report on the Weaver incident found no fault on the part of anyone at the Bureau—either at the scene or at FBI headquarters. Another internal FBI report resulted in minor disciplinary action. FBI higher-ups placed primary blame on Eugene Close, the field commander at Ruby Ridge. As if to illustrate the view that the FBI did not have Vicki Weaver's blood on its hands, Freeh later promoted his close friend Larry Potts, the senior bureau official who supervised the Ruby Ridge operation from Washington, to the position of FBI deputy director.

Agent Close sent a complaint to the Justice Department saying that Potts, not he, was responsible for the new rules of engagement. Rarely does one FBI agent turn on a fellow agent. Yet another investigation caused Director Freeh to suspend five high-ranking FBI officials, including Potts, and to open a criminal investigation three weeks before Specter's scheduled hearings.

Gerry Spence told me he believed those responsible for Vicki and Samuel Weaver's deaths should be tried for murder. He asked Attorney General Reno to prosecute them. She did not appear receptive to the idea, he said.

About three weeks before Specter's hearings began, the government agreed to pay Weaver and his three surviving daughters $3.1 million to settle their civil suit. Spence told the media that the settlement let his clients avoid a trial that would cause them to relive the memories of a "dead mother on the floor for eleven days, rotting in the sun, and a dead boy out in the back in the woodshed." It also avoided a trial that would likely see FBI agents taking the Fifth Amendment and the agency's reputation further sullied.

Randy Weaver was the first witness when the Senate hearings began on September 6. He admitted that he had made a mistake by not showing up for court, even if the date on the notice was incorrect. He looked like the loyal family man the jury found him to be. Yes, he held unpopular views. No, he had no plan to take violent action against Jews or anyone else.

Special Agent Close testified that he had been made the scapegoat for the fiasco. Instead of searching for the truth in its initial internal investigations, he claimed that the Bureau had "twisted" its inquiry to answer one question: "Who do we blame?" Four agents, including the sharpshooter who fired the shot that killed Vicki Weaver, invoked their Fifth Amendment right not to incriminate themselves.

The subcommittee heard from sixty-two witnesses

during fourteen days of hearings and issued a preliminary report a few days before Christmas. The brunt of the criticism was reserved for the FBI.

The preliminary report concluded that although Randy Weaver made mistakes, every federal law enforcement agency involved did so as well. The report pointed out that while the country can tolerate mistakes by people like Weaver, it cannot tolerate serious errors made by federal law enforcement agencies that result in needless human tragedy. It faulted federal officials for flawed intelligence-gathering practices, an unwillingness on the part of some to accept responsibility, and improper internal investigations for the special rules of engagement that told the FBI sharpshooters to shoot any armed adult man even if he was not given a chance to surrender.

Clinton's request for more law enforcement tools to monitor domestic terrorists received a serious setback from the revelations in the Weaver hearings. Many feared Weaver-style abuse, especially against unpopular groups and their followers. Liberals and conservatives from the ACLU to Larry Pratt's Gun Owners of America joined forces to scuttle the administration's antiterrorism legislation.

We must never tolerate misconduct by federal law enforcement agencies. But it is important to remember that they handle thousands of cases every year. Usually, they do their jobs well. Few complain when the FBI brings down Mafia chieftains like John Gotti or when the ATF solves crimes like the World Trade Center bombing. We take everyday law enforcement, like smooth streets, for granted, but complain loudly about a few nasty potholes.

I owe my life to the FBI for infiltrating The Order and warning me of a serious death threat. Over the years, the FBI has apprehended and helped convict twelve people, not counting the twenty-two Order members who have either made threats on my life or my offices, or have been involved in plans to do me and my staff bodily harm. The ATF was primarily responsible for finding and convicting the three men who fire-bombed my offices in 1983. I know that I cannot impartially judge these federal agencies, but I do believe the majority of their agents are honorable men and women dedicated to seeking justice, not imprisoning innocent people.

President George Bush did the nation a great service when he resigned from the National Rifle Association. The organization had described ATF agents as "jack-booted government thugs" who wear "Nazi bucket helmets and black storm trooper uniforms" in a fund-raising letter sent to donors a week before the Oklahoma bombing. In resigning his membership, President Bush wrote, "Your broadside against federal agents deeply offends my own sense of decency and honor, and it offends my concept of service to country."

The fact that lives were lost during both the Waco debacle and the Weaver incident does not make those tragedies morally equivalent to the Oklahoma City bombing as the militias have suggested. Viewing the Waco incident from the perspective of the government's complicity, the deaths were by accident. Viewing the Oklahoma City disaster from the perspective of the bomber's responsibility, the deaths were by design. And even if one were to buy the thoroughly discredited militia line that the government started the blaze that engulfed the Davidians, a crucial distinction would still remain. The FBI pleaded with Koresh and the Davidians to come out of their compound for fifty-one days. The Oklahoma City bombers struck without warning.

The Weaver incident is no more comparable to the Oklahoma City bombing than is Waco. Although there was serious government misconduct throughout the Weaver affair, Randy Weaver could have defused the situation by appearing in court to answer the original charges against him. Instead of doing so, he and his wife inflamed the situation by making threatening statements and by making it clear that Randy would not surrender. Weaver and his wife also used their children to help shield Randy from arrest.

The FBI rules of engagement that directed its sharpshooters to shoot to kill any adult male who was armed surely sanctioned potentially criminal conduct. Drafted in the midst of confusion about the danger the FBI faced atop Ruby Ridge after a U.S. deputy marshal had been killed, the directive called for deadly force even if there was no immediate threat to those at the scene and even if there was no chance that someone posing a serious threat could escape.

But however wrong the FBI directive may have been, it was not simply a matter of revenge for the death of the marshal. After all, the directive gave the government snipers orders to shoot only *armed* men, not unarmed men, women, and children like those in the Oklahoma City federal building. The fact that it applied only to *armed* men demonstrates that the agency was responding to at least a perception of danger from those against whom it contemplated deadly force. The militia fanatics who rail against the New World Order do not even pretend that the Oklahoma City bombers thought that they had anything to worry about from the little children in the Alfred P. Murrah Federal Building.

The Senate report acknowledged that the "events at Ruby Ridge have helped to weaken the bond of trust that must exist between ordinary Americans and our law enforcement agencies." After the Oklahoma City bombing, William Pierce stated that "the bond of trust between the U.S. government and its citizens has been broken." The Senate report said that the "bonds must be reestablished—and that healing must begin with an honest accounting by those in government." Pierce stated that "it's far too late to mend" the bonds.

Far too many people, I'm afraid, agree with Pierce. The shock of the Oklahoma City bombing may have scared away some militia warriors, and the congressional hearings on Waco and Ruby Ridge may have satisfied others. But thousands of self-styled Patriots are still angry with the government and are answering the militia call.

# Gathering Storm

Assessing the magnitude of the threat posed by militia groups operating today is a bit like gauging the risk to shipping posed by icebergs. The number that can be seen is important, but the real danger lies beneath the surface.

From the tips of the icebergs that we can see, it's clear that the militia threat is quite extensive. When we catch a glimpse of what lurks beneath the militia's public front, it's equally clear that the danger is quite extreme.

Between 1994 and 1996, there were at least 441 militia units across the country. Every state had at least one within its borders. Some units have only a few members; others have more than a thousand. In addition to the hundreds of militias that span the country, 368 alllied Patriot groups promoted the formation of militias, provided information and materials to them, or espoused ideas, including Identity doctrines, that are common in militia circles.

The advantage a ship's captain has in assessing iceberg hazards is that one-ninth of an iceberg's mass is always above the water. Militias don't operate on the same law of buoyancy. There is no way that we can detect many of the small militia units or cells that are secretly training in the woods. Militias often shun publicity; they recruit members by word of mouth. There is no requirement that they file with their local chambers of commerce.

Although most militia members may be law-abiding citizens, militia groups attract those with a propensity for violence and act as a springboard for their activities. After a while, angry loners are likely to grow bored roaming the woods and shooting at paper targets. After a while, they are likely to tire of constantly just preparing to take on the New World Order. Like Robert Mathews, they will get fed up with all the talk; they will want action.

As the troops grow restless, militia leaders will hear rumbling behind their backs. They will face competition for members from other militias who portray themselves as "tougher." To keep their followers in line and to maintain their authority—to prove that they have what it takes—militia leaders will be tempted to authorize, or to at least acquiesce in, more and more aggressive operations.

Even if militia leaders hold to the line of strictly defensive training and throw out the renegades, the damage is likely to be done. The militias will have provided access to weaponry and military training. They will also have brought together like-minded people who may embolden one another and go on to form their own secret cell.

Of the 441 militia and 368 Patriot groups that existed between 1994 and 1996, 137 had ties to the racist right—to groups like the Aryan Nations and the Ku Klux Klan. Of all the militias, these groups and the types of members they attract are the most dangerous. As I told

Attorney General Reno six months before the Oklahoma City bombing, "This mixture of armed groups and those who hate is a recipe for disaster."

Over time, the racist world and the militia movement are likely to become concentric circles. In July 1995, approximately two hundred white supremacists and neo-Nazis from around the country and Canada attended the annual Aryan World Congress near Hayden Lake, Idaho. The yearly event is sponsored by the Aryan Nations, the largest neo-Nazi organization in the country, with active members in twenty-two states. Fiery antigovernment speeches promoting militias and revolutionary tactics dominated the gathering. Louis Beam, an Aryan Nations ambassador, urged his followers to join with antigovernment militias and to stockpile weapons. (He also said that my colleagues and I were "lying scum who have to be stopped.")

Behind the scenes of the World Congress, Aryan Nations officials launched an intelligence operation calling for the surveillance of "enemy" groups like civil rights organizations and government agencies. Aryan Nations state offices were instructed to use "SALUTE" reports to collect the intelligence data. SALUTE is an acronym for the type of information to be gathered about the "enemy": size, activity, location, unit, time, and equipment.

Just as the Aryan Nations followers and sympathizers were gathering in Idaho, about two hundred militia activists were gathering in South Dakota for a conference sponsored by the Tri-State Militia, an organization with affiliates in more than twenty states. And just as SALUTE forms were being handed out to Aryan Nations officials, similar SALUTE forms were being distributed to those attending the Tri-State Militia event that same July weekend.

In my years of monitoring the racist right, I have never seen a group use SALUTE forms. In my view, the fact that the Aryan Nations, the largest neo-Nazi organization in the country, and the Tri-State Militia, the nation's largest militia umbrella organization, simultaneously launched similar intelligence-gathering campaigns is more than a coincidence; it is a sign of coordinated action. For those who believe in the possibility of lightning striking twice, consider this: at the same time that the Aryan Nations and the Tri-State Militia were distributing SALUTE forms, the Militia of Montana was asking its membership to gather data using SALUTE forms as well.

Two months after Louis Beam urged the Aryan Nations faithful to join the militia ranks, William Pierce, the author of *The Turner Diaries* and the head of the National Alliance, launched his organization's "Militia Project." His goal for the project is to develop contacts with and to exert influence over militia organizations. As Pierce explained to his members in the September 1995 issue of the *National Alliance Bulletin:*

> Some of the militia groups in the United States are being badly misled in the ideological realm and are in need of some Alliance input. Any member interested in working with a non-Alliance militia group should write to Dr. Pierce, detailing any past or current contacts he has with a militia group and also mentioning any opportunity of which he is aware for establishing a new contact with a militia group in his area.

William Pierce's "Militia Project" comes on the heels of unprecedented growth for his organization. In 1993, he explained that his organization's "[m]embership [had] doubled in 1990–91 and again in 1992. Recruitment rates at the end of 1992 were 30 times what they had been in early 1989." During the past few years, he has been able to get his message out to thousands more by establishing a web site on the Internet (after being on-line for only two months, he reported in 1995 that the site was being accessed by more than five hundred users each day) and by expanding the reach of his radio program, *American Dissident Voices.*

In the aftermath of the Oklahoma City bombing, Pierce pointed out that *The Turner Diaries*—his "Handbook for White Victory"—had been "effective in educating and inspiring a substantial portion of the people who have read it." He predicted more violence: "[W]e will see a much greater incidence of domestic terrorism directed at the government, not just because potential terrorists will draw inspiration from the Oklahoma City bombing, but because the same irritants which led to that bombing can only grow stronger and affect more people with time."

The prospect of more bloodshed is not one that bothers him: "It's a case of either we destroy them or they will destroy us, with no chance for compromise or armistice."

The fervor surrounding the Weaver affair and the Waco disaster continues to be a drawing card for the Patriot cause. *The Jubilee* is sponsoring a major Identity gathering—"Jubilation '96"—for the first weekend of April 1996. In large, bold red letters, the announcement for the meeting states that "Randy Weaver" will be present to answer questions on Ruby Ridge. The announcement also promises that speakers will discuss the "Waco Holocaust" and the Oklahoma City bombing.

The speakers on the Oklahoma City bombing do not intend to mourn the dead. Instead, their goal is to challenge the government's case against Timothy McVeigh and Terry Nichols and to suggest that the government itself was behind the bombing. "What about John Doe 2, 3, 4 and 5?" the announcement reads. "Grand Juror booted for challenging the U.S. prosecution team." "So, where was the ATF? ATF Explosives."

"Three more dynamic speakers" are also slated to appear—Louis Beam, Pete Peters, and Chris Temple. Peters, of course, was the organizer of the 1992 Estes Park meeting that set the agenda for the militia movement. Beam and Temple both spoke there. Along with John Trochmann, Temple founded United Citizens for Justice, the Weaver support group. Beam spoke at its first meeting.

Although only 160 attended the Estes Park meeting, as many as 1,000 of the faithful are expected to attend the April 1996 event.

There will be more people like Robert Mathews and Timothy McVeigh. The militias will give them direction and help them hone their skills. Some of them are probably training now.


At the end of a muddy mountain road, where a small clearing borders a north Idaho creek, Bill Morlin, a Spokane, Wahington, newsman, watches an armed man in camouflage appear out of nowhere.

"He crouches to a shooting position," writes Morlin.

"Seconds later, another masked man carrying a military-style assault rifle steps from behind a clump of pines.

"Four other men in combat gear emerge at the edge of a clearing, holding their rifles and shotguns. . . ."

Morlin was witnessing what few Americans know about, much less see. No law enforcement agent, without the help of an informant, could catch a glimpse of what Morlin and his photographer recorded.

These armed, masked men in full military gear constitute a secret militia cell.

Morlin will not reveal how he was able to interview this secret militia unit. The conditions were stringent. He and a photographer were met at a supermarket parking lot by an intermediary of the unit and drove to a remote mountain site, not the group's usual training area. Both journalists were searched for recording devices. Code names were used. What he saw was "soldiers ready for war."

The modern concept for secret cells of patriot warriors was proposed by Louis Beam in February 1992 in the final issue of his quarterly journal, *The Seditionist*.

Beam had seen the folly of the normal military pyramid organizational plan, with the foot soldiers at the bottom and a leader at each command level to the top. When I sued him and his Knights of the Ku Klux Klan in 1981 to stop their harassment of Vietnamese fishermen in Galveston Bay, it was such a traditional chain of command that destroyed his 2,500-man paramilitary force. A federal court order directed to him, the general of the Klan private army, wrecked the entire operation.

Beam also saw his friends in The Order destroyed in 1984 by a power-hungry and careless leader. When one member of the twenty-five-person band of revolutionaries decided to cooperate with the government to save himself, the FBI was led directly to the top of the organization.

Robert Mathews, the group's leader, as well as many of his lieutenants, had a poorly encoded membership list. The members were compromised and picked off,

one at a time. Beam believed he now had a better organizational structure to oppose the government. He
called it "leaderless resistance."

"The movement for freedom is rapidly approaching
the point," he wrote, "where, for many people, the
option of belonging to a group will be non-existent. . . .
This struggle is rapidly becoming a matter of individual
action, each of its participants making a private decision in the quietness of his heart to resist . . . by any
means necessary. Groups with the pyramid structure
are extremely dangerous . . . when utilized in a resistance movement against state tyranny. . . ." They are
"easy prey for government infiltration, entrapment and
destruction of the personnel involved. The value of [the
secret cell] is that while any one cell can be infiltrated,
exposed or destroyed, such action will have little effect
on the other cells."

The cell structure Beam laid out, and the one Bill
Morlin witnessed, does not have any central control or
direction.

Beam teaches that his "phantom cell" mode of operation needs no one to "issue an order to anyone. Those
truly committed to the cause of freedom will act when
the time is ripe, or will take their cue from others who
precede them." The purpose of leaderless resistance, he
says, "is to defeat state tyranny."

He believes that members of phantom cells, like
McVeigh may have belonged to, don't need a remote
leader to suggest bombing a federal building. They will
"react to objective events in the same way through the
usual tactics of resistance." Patriot newspapers, leaflets,
computers, on-line services, and word of mouth will
keep the true citizen soldier informed of events "allowing a planned response." This response, Beam states,
might be by a lone individual, a "one-man cell."

There is no shortage of far-right information sources giving small clusters of citizen soldiers ideas and inspiration. More than eighty-five newsletters and tabloids go to carefully cultivated mailing lists. The Internet and World Wide Web, accessible to millions simply through a computer and modem, contain more than one hundred web sites ranging from hard-core white supremacists to antigovernment patriots. The topics are current and often inflammatory, including a complete bomb-making guide put on-line within days after the Oklahoma City explosion. Shortwave radio personalities send programs to loyal listeners huddled in small rooms, complete with inflammatory reminders from people like William Pierce: "[We are in] a war for the survival of our race . . . that ultimately we cannot win . . . except by killing our enemies."

Beam's essay, "Leaderless Resistance," is a bold invitation to lawless action, a call to revolution.

> It is clear, therefore, that it is time to rethink traditional strategy and tactics when it comes to opposing a modern police state. America is quickly moving into a long dark night of police state tyranny, where the rights now accepted by most as being inalienable will disappear. Let the coming night be filled with a thousand points of resistance.

"Leaderless Resistance" is the most popular operations manual in militia circles other than *The Turner Diaries*. It was reprinted in *The Jubilee*. It was made a part of the Sacred Warfare Actions Tactics Committee's report at the conclusion of the Estes Park meeting. A short time before Bill Morlin met the Idaho secret cell, it also was reprinted in a popular classified ad tabloid distributed from convenience stores in Coeur d'Alene, Idaho.

\*      \*      \*

Morlin and photographer Dan McComb watch the unnamed militia cell unit don bulletproof vests and begin target practice. Sometimes the cell members shoot at life-size paper targets of Hillary Clinton and FBI agents. They use .308 rifles and powerful telescopes. Long-range sniper shots, said a cell member identifying himself only as No. 6, are the unit's specialty. The tight grouping of bullet holes in the chest of the mock target at one thousand yards is more than enough to qualify for marine expert marksman.

The group, ranging in age from early twenties to fifties, told Morlin they had been training for over two years. Each man paid for his own weapons and equipment, including AR-15s and nine-round military shotguns. A wealthy businessman, No. 3 said, helps finance the ammunition, camping supplies, military gear, travel costs, and high-tech electronic equipment.

Morlin was told by No. 6 that two similar cells existed in northern Idaho. The unit he observed also mentioned a third cell comprised of teenage boys. "They do their own thing, and we haven't given them any military training because we're afraid they'd use it," No. 6 told Morlin. "These kids are products of Weaver and Waco standoffs."

The wooded mountains where Morlin watched the secret cell prepare for guerrilla warfare is an epicenter of militia patriots, especially those with racist and neo-Nazi ties. Within less than a hundred miles is the headquarters of John Trochmann's Militia of Montana, Richard Butler's Aryan Nations compound, Louis Beam's Sandpoint, Idaho, base, and Randy Weaver's Ruby Ridge cabin. The teenage boys in the yet-untrained cell may have been in the crowd shouting insults at FBI agents during the Weaver siege.

The secret cell Morlin observed has no intentions of

allowing government snoopers to foil their training or discover their identity. Morlin reported that the cell members "have camouflage for all seasons and Mylar-layered clothing to avoid infrared scanning aircraft. They use devices called 'electronic ears' which can detect approaching vehicles and other noise." They communicate with a lookout via VHF radio that is as good or better than the equipment used by many police departments.

All this training, No. 6 said, is to defend the area if attacked and to confront federal agents if another Randy Weaver standoff occurs.

Besides the existence of a secret group training to wage guerrilla warfare, the most alarming thing Morlin reported about the group was its willingness to kill law enforcement officers who might attempt to arrest group members. A confrontation with the police might occur while transporting illegal weapons—"traveling hot," No. 3 calls it.

"If we get stopped for a routine traffic incident," the cell member said, "we've got to decide up front if we're going to tolerate that. If we've got a fully automatic rifle or something like that, you have to be thinking, 'If he stops me, I'm going on the offensive.'"

On a hot summer day, small whirlwinds of dust often appear from nowhere on newly planted cotton fields. Clarence Williams, a friend who worked on our farm when I was young, once told me that they were devils fighting. As a small boy, I would watch one gain speed and size as it moved across the field. From nowhere three more would appear like dancing, swirling ballerinas and then, like distant clouds of a gathering storm, the sandy cotton field had countless devil battles.

Predicting when and where militia terrorists will strike next is no easier than guessing when and where the next whirlwind of dust will form. Unfortunately, all that seems certain is that the devils will strike again. And, unfortunately, some of the attacks may be as deadly as the Oklahoma City bombing.

In 1995 alone, over a ton of explosives was stolen from commercial sites in California, Georgia, Indiana, Idaho, and Oklahoma. Dynamite, C-4 plastic explosives, ANFO (ammonium nitrate/fuel oil), raw ammonium nitrate, detonation cord, electric blasting caps, and fuses are now suspected of being in the hands of extremists in the Patriot underground. Somewhere in the Smoky Mountains, law enforcement sources believe, there is a hidden cache of Stinger missiles, LAW rockets, explosives, machine guns, and thousands of rounds of military-grade ammunition.

Just days after the Oklahoma City tragedy, government agents uncovered a plot to blow up the federal courthouse in Spokane, Washington, with a fertilizer bomb. Darwin Michael Gray, the man charged, was a supporter and longtime friend of Randy Weaver. The building he planned to bomb contained the office of agents who investigated the Weaver standoff. He eventually pleaded guilty.

A month later, Larry Harris, who has ties to white supremacist groups and is a militia sympathizer, was arrested in Lancaster, Ohio, for allegedly buying bubonic plague bacteria by mail from a food-testing laboratory. Police found the freeze- dried bacteria, hand grenade triggers, homemade explosives, and detonating fuses in Harris's residence. Harris pleaded guilty to one charge of wire fraud in connection with his purchase of the bacteria.

Charles Polk, a tax protester who authorities say has

ties to an antigovernment militia, was indicted by a federal grand jury for plotting to blow up an IRS building in Austin, Texas. Prosecutors say he was trying to purchase plastic explosives at the time of his arrest in September. They also say he had a stockpile of sixty weapons, including an AK-47.

In the beginning of December, three members of the Oklahoma Constitutional Militia were arrested in a plot to bomb my office as well as the Houston branch of the Anti-Defamation League. They were charged with mixing an Oklahoma City–type fertilizer bomb just moments before they were arrested.

The terrorist plot that was potentially the most deadly was exposed at the end of December 1995. It began in 1993 with the arrest of Thomas Lavy, age fifty-four. Canadian authorities confiscated a can of white powder as Lavy crossed a border checkpoint coming from Alaska. He had $80,000 in cash when arrested. He made bail and fled.

Chemists determined the powder was ricin, one of the most deadly poisons known. It is made from common castor beans. A mere speck of ricin on the sharp tip of an umbrella was used by Soviet agents to kill a Bulgarian defector, George Markov, on a London sidewalk in 1978. Scientists say it is six thousand times as potent as cyanide and twelve thousand times more deadly than rattlesnake venom.

Lavy was located by federal agents in an isolated stone cabin in the remote wilderness of northern Arkansas. The cabin was not far from the bunker where Gordon Kahl hid out while a fugitive or from the former headquarters of the neo-Nazi group the Covenant, Sword and Arm of the Lord. Some forty FBI agents and army chemical warfare specialists from Aberdeen, Maryland, surrounded the cabin. Lavy was apprehended on December 20, 1995, without incident. He was charged under antiterrorism statutes with possession of 130 grams of ricin. During a search of Lavy's cabin, agents found a tin canister filled with raw castor beans and a recipe for producing ricin.

Stone County, Arkansas, sheriff Fred Black said Lavy's neighbors claimed that he had ties to area "survivalist groups." Federal authorities were anxious to find out who might have been working with Lavy and to whom he may have given the deadly poison. Two members of the Minnesota Patriots Council, a militia cell, were convicted in March on charges that they planned to use ricin to kill federal employees.

Thomas Lavy will not be telling anyone his contacts or his plans. He hung himself in his Arkansas jail cell two days before Christmas.

On December 7, 1995, Private James Burmeister drove into a mostly black neighborhood in Fayetteville, North Carolina, near his Fort Bragg army base seeking blacks to assassinate, prosecutors claim. Two other soldiers accompanied him. He allegedly found Jackie Burden, twenty-seven, and Michael James, thirty-six, and taunted them with racial slurs before shooting them in the head with a semiautomatic handgun. Both died instantly. The three soldiers were charged with murder. Burmeister had copies of racist material in his off-base home. He could be a member of a secret group operating around military bases.

The clandestine group, the Special Forces Underground, is buried deep on the fringes of America's military. We learned of the group's existence shortly before the Oklahoma City bombing through postings on the American Patriot Fax Network. Formed at Fort Bragg, North Carolina, on August 23, 1992, during the height of the FBI's siege of Randy Weaver's cabin, the group's goal is to force the federal government "back into its constitutional prison." It relies primarily on active-duty military personnel and ex-servicemen with covert operations training. The organization expresses little faith in the aboveground militia groups: "[T]he Patriot Movement in general and militia groups in particular need to get a firm grip on the realities of resistance and underground operations." The Pentagon has launched an investigation.

Bill Morlin witnessed three hours of intense military-type training by men willing to die for their beliefs. No. 6 told Morlin that "my wife supports me 100 percent. She'd rather have my bloody head in her lap than to have me fail to uphold my principles." The day's training complete, the small group faded away down the muddy road, vanishing into the woods.

They appeared and departed just like Louis Beam envisioned when he wrote about secret cells and leaderless resistance—"like the fog which forms when conditions are right and disappears when they are not."

# The Last
# Best Hope

The threat we face from militia extremists today reminds me of an incident back in my hometown of Mount Meigs, Alabama, when I was twelve. A family had moved into a large, old frame house next to my uncle's grocery store. They had boys ranging in age from six to eighteen who kept our otherwise peaceful community in constant turmoil.

The Coca-Cola sign on my uncle's store porch was peppered with rocks one night, scaring my grandmother who lived next door. Things turned up missing: a spare tire, a gun kept in the feed store, and a new pair of overalls from my aunt's clothesline. Suspicions pointed to the new family, but we had no proof.

One day, the oldest boy in this white family picked a fight with a black youth half his size. Beat the dickens out of him for no good reason we could see. A week later, the youngest boy poured kerosene on a dog that hung out by the blacksmith's shop and set him on fire. The burning dog yelped and howled as he raced down the gravel road. My grandmother, who was sitting on her porch, saw the whole thing.

She ran to my uncle's store. He'd heard the commotion, people screaming at the boy for lighting up the dog and others chasing the animal trying to save its life.

"What's a body gonna do?" my grandmother asked. I can still see the fear in her small watery blue eyes as I recall the day.

"We gonna call the law," my uncle answered. "These bullies got no place in Mount Meigs." The sheriff came, the family of troublemakers eventually moved on, and Mount Meigs returned to normal.

Our national community was shocked by the Oklahoma City tragedy. Few want to face another such crisis. Like my grandmother, we want to know what to do.

No one can guarantee that some small group of terrorists will not slip through whatever protective measures we devise. But that does not mean we are helpless to deal with the threat that we face. There is a large, extended, unruly family in our community. It's time to call the law.

These bullies have a track record we cannot ignore. And what they have been accused of in the past is happening today.

Louis Beam and eleven racist leaders were charged in 1987 with planning to poison water supplies, sabotage railroads, and bomb federal buildings.

The plan was part of an alleged conspiracy to overthrow the federal government. Prosecutors lost the case. The defendants convinced the all-white jury that they were, if anything, only exercising their free speech rights.

Today federal offices and buildings have been bombed, plans to poison water supplies and people have been stopped, large weapons and explosives stockpiles seized, and plans to destroy telephone relay centers, airports, and bridges exposed.

Private paramilitary groups, small cells of far-right terrorists, and militias are believed involved in each incident. They weren't just exercising their right to free speech. They were causing or planning to cause death and destruction.

William Pierce, seeing his *Turner Diaries* fictional bombing plot turned into reality in Oklahoma City, told his nationwide radio audience a few days after the bombing that things "will become worse."

> Should we sit on our hands and watch the government terrorists and the private terrorists fight it out? That, unfortunately, is what most of us have been doing until now. I believe that it is time for a few of us to begin shouldering a little responsibility for what's going on in the world around us.

Some will interpret his call for action in political terms. But others, like Timothy McVeigh, who slavishly follow *The Turner Diaries*, might fulfill Pierce's radio prophecy that "citizens [will] strike back and engage in terrorism against the government."

Louis Beam told his audience at Estes Park that the murder of Randy Weaver's wife and son would only whet the tyrant's appetite.

> If federal terrorism goes unchallenged, then no one in this nation is safe. Government terrorism, if ignored, does not go away, but gets worse. Like a lion having tasted the blood of human victims, they will come for more, new victims.

I am more concerned with the victims of militia terrorists than with FBI or ATF excesses. I do not for a moment condone the FBI's handling of the Weaver incident. I also have some reservations about the ATF's Waco strategy. But these federal agencies have a legal basis to exist and can be harshly dealt with for their improper actions.

Unregulated private armies have no legal basis. Their threat is real. We cannot be timid or tardy when dealing with this danger.

While the Constitution of the United States protects the right of people like William Pierce and Louis Beam to say and write what they please, it does not give anyone the right to form a private army or to engage in military maneuvers in a secret cell. The Second Amendment provides that "[a] well regulated Militia, being necessary to the security of a free State, the right of the people to keep and bear Arms, shall not be infringed." Courts have always held that the amendment protects only state-sponsored "well regulated militias" from undue federal interference. It does not provide a constitutional right of individual gun ownership. Although some legal commentators maintain that the past judicial decisions interpreting the Second Amendment in this manner are wrong, most scholars agree with the courts that the Constitution's "right to bear arms" applies only to members of official state militias acting in their official capacity, not to unregulated individual citizens.

Warren Burger, a former chief justice of the United States and a conservative jurist at that, called the gun lobby's interpretation of the Second Amendment "one of the greatest pieces of fraud, I repeat the word 'fraud,' on the American public by special interest groups that I've ever seen in my lifetime.

"The real purpose of the Second Amendment was to ensure that the state armies—the militias—would be maintained for the defense of the state," said Burger.

"The very language of the Second Amendment refutes any argument that it was intended to guarantee every citizen an unfettered right to any kind of weapon he or she desires."

No less a hero to the militia movement than George Washington, the Father of our country, denounced the actions of privately armed groups with a political agenda as a threat to democratic society. He then went out and crushed the Whiskey Rebellion.

Given that there is no constitutional right to individual gun ownership, there is obviously no right to go one step further and have a private army under the Second Amendment. The Supreme Court made this point clear back in 1886. "Military organization and military drill and parade under arms are subjects especially under the control of the government of every country. They cannot be claimed as a right independent of law. Under our political system they are subject to the . . . regulation and control of the state and federal governments, acting in due regard to their respective prerogatives and powers."

The First Amendment likewise does not give anyone the right to form a private army or to engage in dangerous paramilitary training. The amendment guarantees the right to peaceably assemble to express one's views, no matter how unpopular, controversial, or repulsive those views may be. But the government may impose limits on the time, place, and manner of such expression. The government, for example, could prohibit demonstrators from using loud bullhorns in residential neighborhoods in order to protect the peace and tranquillity of the residents. In a similar manner, the government can insist that those who assemble do so without automatic weapons in order to protect against a potential deadly breach of the peace. Such a restriction would leave those involved in the Patriot movement perfectly free to come together to make all the speeches they want about their hatred of the government.

Most states have laws that ban private militias completely or at least prevent them from training others to commit violence. Antimilitia laws, on the books in twenty-four states, are the most sweeping state laws that apply to militias. They ban all private military organizations except those authorized by the state. Anti–paramilitary training laws prohibit private paramilitary training with weapons or explosives when carried out with the knowledge or intent that the training will be used in a civil disorder. Twenty-four states, including seven with antimilitia laws, have anti–paramilitary training laws.

The two types of state laws operate somewhat differently. Anti–paramilitary training laws typically ban such traihing only in the limited circumstances when those involved know or intend that a civil disorder will result from their activities. Antimilitia laws, on the other hand, ban *all* unauthorized militias, regardless of whether the participants have any specific criminal intent or knowledge. Antimilitia laws generally require a showing that a group of people associated together in a formal military-type organization. Anti–paramilitary training statutes, by contrast, can be used against groups as small as two or three people.

Our cases have proved that these laws can work. In Texas, we used the state antimilitia statute to close down the paramilitary camps operated by the Ku Klux Klan under Louis Beam's direction. In ruling that the camps were illegal, the court defined military organizations in a way that distinguished Scouts and hunters from heavily armed men preparing for a battle. In North Carolina, we used that state's paramilitary law to enjoin the White Patriot Party from operating as a paramilitary organization.

Outside of the cases we have brought, the state laws against militia and paramilitary activity have almost never been enforced. In an effort to address this problem, I wrote letters to the state attorneys general across the nation less than a month after the Oklahoma City bombing urging them to use their state laws to put an end to unauthorized militia activity. In those states that did not have applicable laws, I asked the attorneys general to sponsor antimilitia and anti–paramilitary training legislation.

So far, the reaction to our call for state action has been disappointing. Some state prosecutors still labor under the mistaken assumption that the Constitution somehow gives people the right to have a private army. In response to my letter, the West Virginia attorney general said that banning private militias was "a very touchy area because of the First Amendment right of people to associate." Likewise, the Colorado attorney general wrote that "we must be cautious, that in our zeal to protect citizens of this state, we do not repress dissent with which we disagree. . . . I am sure you would agree that such dissent must always be allowed and protected under the First Amendment." Similarly, the attorney general of North Dakota responded by saying that "we have to be careful not to close access to free speech and deny people the right to change the system. A worse situation may be created. It is inappropriate to label people based on group membership. We cannot act on that basis. We have to focus on behavior, not beliefs. Everyone is entitled to their beliefs; that is what makes America great."

But engaging in paramilitary activity is "behavior, not beliefs." Banning private armies does not deprive anyone of their "beliefs," only their opportunity to wreak havoc. Paramilitary activity is not "what makes America great." It is what makes America dangerous. While militia members have a First Amendment right to believe and say whatever they please, they have no right to engage in military maneuvers.

Despite the fact that the Oklahoma City tragedy came with little warning, some state prosecutors have taken the view that antimilitia laws should not be enforced or enacted because the militias in their states are supposedly harmless. In rejecting my call for vigorous enforcement of state laws, the South Dakota attorney general said that he was "not interested in leaving the impression that we [the state prosecutors' office] think there are a bunch of crazies running around South Dakota." He assured the public, "That is not the case."

Two and a half months later, two hundred militia activists from around the country gathered near Gregory, South Dakota, under the auspices of the Tri-State Militia, a national militia umbrella organization headquartered there. During the meeting, the group launched a campaign to gather intelligence on military and other targets using SALUTE forms. That same weekend, the Aryan Nations secretly distributed SALUTE forms at its annual Aryan World Congress.

Two weeks later, according to federal officials, the leader of the Oklahoma Constitutional Militia and one of his associates met with members of the Tri-State Militia to solicit their help in bombing several buildings, including my office in Montgomery. Although members of the Tri-State Militia claim that they blew the whistle on the plotters, I can't help but feel that we would all be safer if the South Dakota attorney general took the militia threat a bit more seriously.

It would be interesting to see the reaction of the

state attorneys general if the militia groups operating today were all located near large metropolitan cities like Detroit or Philadelphia, and were comprised only of blacks. If law enforcement's violent reaction to the Black Panthers of the 1960s is any example, I seriously doubt if black militia units training with assault weapons, distributing recipes for building bombs, and preaching hatred of government would be tolerated.

In many areas of the country, there is tremendous political pressure on local law enforcement officials to turn a blind eye to the reality of the militia threat. Militia members and their sympathizers make up a significant and vocal portion of numerous local electorates. Rural sheriffs who can count votes may be all too willing to buy the line that the militia is just like a big "neighborhood watch."

Fear is also a factor. Law enforcement officials remember how three of their own were killed when they tried to arrest Gordon Kahl, the tax protester and Posse Comitatus member from North Dakota. They remember how a federal marshal lost his life on Ruby Ridge during the Randy Weaver affair. Many have received or heard about threats of violence from militia members. Indeed, many are outgunned by their local militias.

Whenever a local law enforcement official is reluctant to enforce state laws against unauthorized militias or paramilitary training, the entire country is at risk. The Oklahoma City bombing suspects met with a militia in Michigan and assembled their bomb in Kansas. Timothy McVeigh may have had ties to a small patriot cell in Arizona. Willie Ray Lampley, the leader of the Oklahoma Constitutional Militia, met with members of the Tri-State Militia in South Dakota and has been charged with conspiring to blow up my office in

Alabama and an Anti-Defamation League office in
Texas.

To prevent the failure of local law enforcement officials to create safe havens that private militias can use
to strike out at other areas of the country, each state
should set up a special task force to respond to militia
activity. Because action even at the state level may be
inadequate, the federal government also must have the
tools with which to respond. The current federal
anti–paramilitary training statute punishes only those
who instruct others in fomenting civil disorder. The
statute should be amended to punish trainees as well.
In addition, a federal statute should be enacted that
prohibits private militias that are not authorized by the
states. By exempting any state-authorized militias from
its reach, such a statute would not infringe on a state's
right to maintain a "well regulated militia" under the
Second Amendment.

Federal legislation regulating the dissemination of
dangerous substances like ammonium nitrate that can
be used to make explosives or weapons of mass destruction should also be enacted. Although there may be a
First Amendment right to publish directions for making
destructive devices, no one has an unfettered right to
manufacture or buy dynamite.

To limit militia access to military training and
weapons, the Department of Defense should prohibit
military personnel from any involvement in militia
activity. Members of the armed services who violate the
prohibition should face the prospect of discharge. No
known militia members should be allowed to enlist in
the armed forces.

During our case against the White Patriot Party in
North Carolina, we documented the fact that marines
from Camp Lejeune were involved with the neo-Nazi

group's paramilitary force. I immediately wrote Caspar Weinberger, then the Secretary of Defense, and asked him to prohibit active-duty members of the armed services from holding membership in groups like the Klan and taking part in their activities.

In response, the Defense Department issued a directive giving military commanders the authority to take disciplinary action against military personnel who participate in the activities of white supremacist or neo-Nazi groups. The directive stated that "Military Personnel, duty bound to uphold the Constitution, must reject participation in such organizations. Active participation, including public demonstrations, recruiting and training members, and organizing or leading such organizations, is utterly incompatible with military service. The system of rank and command, the requirements of trust and cohesiveness among service members, and the discipline essential to military units demand that service personnel reject the goals of such groups." The same can be said for participation in militia organizations.

Law enforcement agencies cannot do their jobs effectively if their ranks continue to include members of the militias that they should be policing. For this reason, law enforcement departments at every level of government should also prohibit their members from participating in militia activities. This should include state National Guards.

In those states that have antimilitia statutes, such a prohibition obviously would not raise any legal difficulties. Indeed, in states with antimilitia laws, law enforcement agencies already have the authority to kick out officers who are militia members. In those states that do not currently have antimilitia laws, such a prohibition would still be lawful given that no one has a constitutional right to be a member of a private army.

Without good information, law enforcement will never be in a position to respond adequately to the militia threat. Presently, the Militia Task Force at the Southern Poverty Law Center—a group of less than ten people—knows more about the militia world than the FBI. This situation must change.

As law enforcement agencies gather data on militia activities, a balance must be struck between our security needs and our First Amendment freedoms. We should never forget the FBI's excesses during the civil rights and Vietnam protest eras. We must protect our privacy. But if the law allows the police to keep track of explosives, there is no reason why it should not also allow the police to keep track of people who advocate blowing up buildings. Federal and state authorities should be allowed to maintain data from *publicly* available sources on those who call for violence even if their rhetoric does not amount to illegal incitement and even if it is couched in terms of "self-defense."

Law enforcement agencies also must do a much better job sharing information. The Patriot world is linked through the Internet, numerous publications, telephone-fax trees, and computer bulletin boards. Law enforcement officials in one county often don't know what those in the next county are doing.

One of the most difficult questions to answer is whether cracking down on the militias will spur violent reactions from them. In his radio address following the Oklahoma City bombing, Pierce predicted just such a dynamic.

> More and more, the government will lash out at dissidents, at anyone who is not politically correct.

And the two sides will feed on each other. The more repressive and terroristic the government becomes, the more individuals there will be who will engage in terrorism to get back at the government. And the more individual terrorism there is against the government, the more terroristic the government will become, in turn.

Such fears were also expressed by state attorneys general in response to my call for state action against the militias. The California attorney general wrote that he was "concerned that attempts to create new laws making personal association with such groups a crime . . . will only increase their suspicion and agitation toward the government in general and law enforcement officers in particular." The North Dakota attorney general expressed the view that a "worse situation may be created" if she enforced her state's antimilitia law because it might "deny people the right to change the system."

But in our democracy, people have "the right to change the system" at the ballot box, not at the barrel of a gun. While law enforcement should never needlessly antagonize anyone—especially frustrated people with deadly weapons—we cannot allow our fear of lawbreakers to stop us from enforcing the law. We cannot allow ourselves to be blackmailed in this fashion.

I say this fully aware of the risks involved. After we shut down Louis Beam's paramilitary force in Texas, our offices were burned, and The Order targeted me for assassination. After we challenged the White Patriot Party's paramilitary operations in court, members of that neo-Nazi organization conspired to kill me and blow up our offices. I know that vigorous law enforcement action against the militias will have its costs.

But the cost of not moving firmly will be higher. Had we and the state attorney general not stood up to Beam in Texas, he and his fellow Klansmen would have driven the Vietnamese fishermen out of Galveston Bay. Had we and the United States attorney in North Carolina not forced Glenn Miller's private army out of business, the C-4 plastic explosives they obtained from a military base would have been used to blow up a power dam or destroy a school bus filled with black children. Timidity in the face of the threat of terror is likely to invite even more terror. Unless the schoolyard bully is stopped or changed, no child on the playground is safe. Ignoring a bully only encourages him.

As long as there is hatred in our midst, acts of inhumanity will be with us. But, as Dr. Martin Luther King reminded us, we should "never succumb to the temptation of believing that legislation and judicial decrees play only minor roles. . . . Morality cannot be legislated, but behavior can be regulated. Judicial decrees may not change the heart, but they can restrain the heartless."

After the focus shifted from foreign to domestic terrorists following the Oklahoma City bombing, I was invited to appear on a number of major news shows. My letter to Attorney General Reno six months before the explosion warning of militia hate groups, and our long history of fighting private racist armies, prompted these invitations. My appearances prompted an extremely large number of letters.

Most critical letters came from well-meaning citizens fearful of government, uninformed of the dangerous men manipulating the militias and confused about the legal right of private armies to operate.

If we start legislating against paramilitary training, just how do we treat the Boy Scouts, our mili-

against people on the basis of their sex. I have sued state and county governments over thirty-five times for violating citizens' rights.

But whenever I have gone into court against the government, I have always relied on the document that established the system of government itself—the United States Constitution. It is the document that gave Randy Weaver the right to sue the government for killing his wife and son. It is the document that gave the Congress of the United States the authority to investigate the blunders that led to the fiery deaths of the Branch Davidians at Waco. It is the document that gave us, through our elected representatives, the power to impeach the most powerful person on earth, the president of the United States, the man whose IRS minions harassed me.

One of the great ironies of the current climate of government mistrust is that it is occurring at a time when the government is undergoing fundamental changes. Six months before the Oklahoma City bombing, voters went to the polls and repudiated forty years of Democratic Party hegemony. To the extremists of the Patriot movement, of course, the change means nothing. Like George Wallace a generation ago, they see no difference between the major political parties. But the average person who comes to a Michigan Militia meeting is someone who is concerned about his or her community, someone who usually votes. While that person may be frustrated with the pace of changes, he surely feels that he has good reasons to vote the way he does. We need to remind those who are understandably frustrated with the government that there are peaceful ways to fight for change. We need to ensure that avenues for dissent remain open. While most of those involved in the Patriot movement may believe with William Pierce that the "bond of trust between the U.S. government and its citizens has been broken," we must convince them that people like Pierce are wrong when they claim that "it's far too late to mend" that bond.

Another great irony of the current situation is that the antigovernment flames are being fanned the hardest by those who are living proof that our system of government works. However much government officials may have wanted to see Louis Beam convicted of plotting against the government, a jury in Fort Smith, Arkansas, set him free. Today, the First Amendment protects him as he goes around the country promoting leaderless resistance. The same First Amendment protects Pierce as he fans the flames of hate from his Hillsboro, West Virginia, mountain compound. One need only look to the pages of the *National Alliance Bulletin* to understand the type of dissent that people like Pierce would tolerate if they could remake America.

> Those who speak against us now should be looked at as dead men—as men marching in lockstep toward their own graves—rather than as persons to be feared or respected or given any consideration.

Of course, we should never forget that government officials—precisely because they are ordinary people with extraordinary powers—have engaged and will engage in serious abuses. We should always insist that they be held accountable for their misconduct, that any breach of the public trust be redressed. Those who cover up wrongdoing should be dealt with in an especially firm manner because their actions threaten the ability of our system of government to correct itself.

More important than faith in the Constitution is faith in the American people. We must remember that most of those involved in the Patriot movement are good Americans. They simply have gripes against the government. Most of us probably share a number of their views.

We must try to separate the persons attracted to the Patriot movement from those who would exploit their anger. We must appeal to their common sense and decency. When militia leaders like Norman Olson make absurd claims like the Japanese government was behind the Oklahoma City bombing, the local media should publicize their statements, not ignore them. When militia advocates like Pete Peters offer twisted, anti-Semitic interpretations of the Bible, the local clergy should counter them. The links between the militia movement and the white supremacist, neo-Nazi world should be exposed.

We also must have the courage—blacks and whites, liberals and conservatives—to apply the same standards to all racists. Some claim that while black people may be prejudiced, they cannot be racists. Racism, the argument goes, requires power—an ability to impose one's will on another—a commodity that black people supposedly do not possess.

This argument is as silly as it is wooden. When black politicians dominate many of our nation's largest cities, when one of the major political parties flirts with drafting a black man to run for our country's highest office, when black entertainers and sports figures play prominent roles in our cultural life, it is ludicrous to claim that African-Americans have no power. When Nation of Islam leader Louis Farrakhan calls Jews "bloodsuckers," he is marching lockstep with neo-Nazi leaders like Dr. William Pierce. All are racists.

Reverend Jesse Jackson and other black leaders held hands with Dr. Martin Luther King and sang "black and white together, we shall overcome." They later stood shoulder-to-shoulder with Farrakhan in his Million Man March despite his call for the creation of a separate black nation within America. Many feared being branded race traitors if they repudiated this demagogue. These leaders—and President Clinton—tried to distinguish the message of hope for black males from the messenger's hatred for whites.

This same logic would forgive German leaders for standing with Adolf Hitler as he railed against the poor economic condition of workers, *Mein Kampf* notwithstanding. Blacks, Jews, and the mainstream media would be outraged if our president addressed a gathering called by William Pierce or Louis Beam, even if some of their issues, like Ruby Ridge, had some merit. It is this type of hypocrisy that undermines faith in our system and lends credibility to the Patriot movement.

In our country's darkest hour, President Lincoln said that our democracy was "the last, best hope of earth." Our Constitution was drafted by men, not handed down by God to any one race. While we face tough choices in the years ahead, we must remember that the give-and-take of the democratic process is essential to the health of our nation. We must respect each person's point of view and work to ensure that everyone has the opportunity to play a meaningful role in the life of our nation. But there is no place in the debate for those who would impose their views on others at gunpoint.

True patriots are in voting lines, not militia columns, doing their part to ensure the continuation of our democratic way of life.

# Source Notes

A lot of good writers have done excellent reporting on many aspects of and many of the people involved with the Patriot and militia movements. I want to thank and acknowledge those writers whose work I drew upon in writing *Gathering Storm*. This list is by no means complete. It is simply an attempt to indicate the principal published works consulted for this book.

## BOOKS

Carter, Dan T. *The Politics of Rage: George Wallace, the Origins of the New Conservatism, and the Transformation of American Politics.* New York: Simon and Schuster, 1995.

Coates, James. *Armed and Dangerous: The Rise of the Survivalist Right.* New York: Noonday Press, 1987.

Corcoran, James. *Bitter Harvest: The Birth of Paramilitary Terrorism in the Heartland.* New York: Viking Penguin, 1990, 1995.

Dees, Morris, and Steve Fiffer. *A Season for Justice: The Life and Times of Civil Rights Lawyer Morris Dees.* New York: Scribners, 1991.

———. *Hate on Trial: The Case Against America's Most Dangerous Neo-Nazi.* New York: Villard, 1993.

Flynn, Kevin, and Gary Gerhardt. *The Silent Brotherhood: Inside America's Racist Underground.* New York: Free Press, 1989.

Gibson, James William. *Warrior Dreams: Paramilitary Culture in Post-Vietnam America.* New York: Hill and Wang, 1994.

Hacker, Andrew. *Two Nations: Black and White, Separate, Hostile and Unequal.* New York: Scribners, 1992.

Pierce, William [Andrew Macdonald]. *The Turner Diaries.* Hillsboro, West Virginia: National Vanguard Books, 1978.

Robertson, Pat. *The New World Order.* Dallas: Word Publishing, 1991.

Spence, Gerry. *From Freedom to Slavery: The Birth of Tyranny in America.* New York: St. Martin's Press, 1993.

Stanton, Bill. *Klanwatch: Bringing the Ku Klux Klan to Justice.* New York: Grove Weidenfeld, 1991.

Walter, Jess. *Every Knee Shall Bow.* New York: ReganBooks, 1995.


ARTICLES

Beam, Louis. "Leaderless Resistance." *The Seditionist*, Feb. 1992.

———. "For Whom the Bells Toll." *The Jubilee*, May/June 1995.

Bendavid, Naftali. "NRA Paramilitary Link Sparks Controversy in Wake of Bombing." *The Recorder*, May 3, 1995.

Berke, Richard L. "U.S. Voters Focus on Selves, Poll Says." *New York Times*, Sept. 21, 1994.

Berlet, Chip. "The Right Rides High." *The Progressive*, Oct. 1994.

Biema, David Van. "Militias." *Time*, June 26, 1995.

Butterworth, Fox. "Long Before Bombing, Gun Lobby Was Lashing Out at Federal Agents." *New York Times*, May 8, 1995.

Cooper, Marc. "The Paranoid Style." *The Nation*, Apr. 10, 1995.

———. "Camouflage Days, E-mail Nights. Militias." *The Nation*, Oct. 23, 1995.

Corcoran, James. "A Lesson Forgotten in Waco Assault." *Boston Globe* (Focus), Mar. 7, 1993.

Covington, Harold. "An Open Letter to Morris Seligman Dees." *Resistance*, June 1995.

Cushman, Erik. "Crime and Punishment." *The Missoula Independent*, Mar. 23, 1995.

DeRosa, Robin. "Tuning in to High-Wattage Talk Show Host." *USA Today*, Feb. 1, 1995.

"The Echoes of Ruby Ridge." *Newsweek*, Aug. 28, 1995.

Egan, Timothy. "Trying to Explain Support for Paramilitary Groups." *New York Times*, May 2, 1995.

"The Face of Terror." *Time*, May 1, 1995.

Farrell, John Aloysius, and Diego Ribadeneira. "Skill, Luck and Legwork: On the Trail of the Suspects." *Boston Globe*, Apr. 23, 1995.

Fineman, Howard. "Friendly Fire." *Newsweek*, May 8, 1995.

Foster, Jim. "Agents List Ingredients for Alleged Explosives." *Muskogee Daily Phoenix*, Nov. 14, 1995.

Fuson, Ken. "Randy Weaver; He's a Rallying Cry for the Far Right but a Reluctant Symbol." *New York Times*, Aug. 27, 1995.

Gordon, Marcy. "Angry Militia Leaders Testify; Law Officials Condemn Groups." Associated Press, June 15, 1995.

Hackworth, David H., and Peter Annin. "The Suspect Speaks Out." *Newsweek*, July 3, 1995.

Hawkins, Beth. "Chronicling the Growth of a Movement." *Detroit Metro Times*, Oct. 12, 1994.

Hendricks, Mike. "I Lost My Job . . . Americans Cry: All This Must Stop." *Kansas City Star*, Nov. 26, 1995.

Herbert, Bob. "Militia Madness." *New York Times*, June 7, 1995.

Holmes, Steven A. "Terror in Oklahoma: Gun Laws; Bombing Alters the Landscape for Gun Lobby." *New York Times*, Apr. 28, 1995.

"How Dangerous Are They? An Inside Look at America's Antigovernment Zealots." *Time*, May 8, 1995.

Jacoby, Mary. "How Gun Owners Call Shots in a Hill Office." *Roll Call*, Oct. 26, 1995.

Johnson, Dirk. "Conspiracy Theories' Impact Reverberates in Legislature." *New York Times*, July 6, 1995.

Jorgensen, Leslie. "AM Armies." *EXTRA*, Mar./Apr. 1995.

Junas, Daniel. "Rise of Citizen Militias—Angry White Guys with Guns." *Covert Action Quarterly*, Spring 1995.

Kelley, Donna. "Text of Senate Hearings on Militias, Part 1." CNN, June 15, 1995.

Kelly, Michael. "The Road to Paranoia." *The New Yorker*, June 19, 1995.

Kifner, John. "Door-to-Door with Collection of Photos, Agents Scour an Arizona Town for Bombing Clues." *New York Times*, May 6, 1995.

———. "Bomb Suspect Felt at Home Riding the Gun-Show Circuit." *New York Times*, July 5, 1995.

———. "A Puzzle Unfinished." *New York Times*, Aug. 13, 1995.

———. "Oklahoma Bomb Suspect: Unraveling of Frayed Life." *New York Times*, Dec. 31, 1995.

Kovaleski, Serge F. "'One World' Conspiracies Prompt Montana Militia's Call to Arms." *Washington Post*, Apr. 29, 1995.

LaCayo, Richard. "Anatomy of a Disaster; A Settlement Avoids a Court Case, but the Crisis over Ruby Ridge Continues." *New York Times*, Aug. 28, 1995.

Lardner, George, Jr., and Pierre Thomas. "U.S. to Pay Family in FBI Idaho Raid." *Washington Post*, Aug. 16, 1995.

Larson, Erik. "AFT Under Siege." *Time*, July 24, 1995.

———. "Unrest in the West." *Time,* Oct. 23, 1995.

Lewis, Neil. "Clinton Plan Would Let FBI Infiltrate Menacing Groups." *New York Times*, Apr. 25, 1995.

———. "Commander at Idaho Standoff Calls FBI Inquiry Cover-up." *New York Times*, Sept. 20, 1995.

Martelle, Scott. "Going to Extremes." *The Detroit News*, May 17, 1995.

McFadden, Robert D. "A Life of Solitude and Obsessions." *New York Times*, May 4, 1995.

McPhee, Michael R. "Police Cite Potential, Pride in Routine Work." *Boston Globe*, Apr. 23, 1995.

Metzger, Tom. "Setting the Stage." *WAR*, July 1995.

"Militias in America 1995." Institute for Alternative Journalism. 1995.

Mintz, John. "Militias Meet the Senate with Conspiracies to Share; Leaders Sound Off on Oklahoma." *Washington Post*, June 16, 1995.

Morlin, Bill. "Agents Deny Weaver Set Up." *Spokane Spokesman-Review*, Sept. 8, 1995.

Niewert, David. "Phone Interview with Bo Gritz." Pacific Rim News Service, Nov. 10, 1994.

"Oklahoma Indictments." *New York Times*, Aug. 12, 1995.

Pates, Mikkel. "Militia Members Call Deadly Bombing an Atrocity." *The Forum of Fargo-Moorhead*, Apr. 22, 1995.

"Patriots and Profits." CNN Special Report, Oct. 29, 1995.

Phillips, Leslie. "Talk Show Hosts Crank Up the Political Volume." *USA Today*, Oct. 26, 1994.

———. "Terror in Oklahoma: The Far Right, New Medium for the Far Right." *USA Today*, Apr. 26, 1995.

Pressley, Sue Ann. "For a Freshman, Lessons About Limelights and Lightning Rods." *Washington Post*, June 25, 1995.

Purdum, Todd. "Clinton Seeks Broad Powers in Battle Against Terrorism: Oklahomans Mourn Their Loss." *New York Times*, Apr. 24, 1995.

"The Ragged Edge." Series by staff of *Spokane Spokesman-Review*, Dec. 3, 4, 10, 11, 1995.

Read, Richard. "Oregon's Militia Lying Low." *The Oregonian*, June 6, 1995.

Reavis, Dick, J. "What Really Happened at Waco." *Texas Monthly*, July 1995.

"Reno Defends Waco Raid, Rejects Parallel." *Boston Globe* (Reuters), May 6, 1995.

*The Resister*. Official publication of the Special Forces Underground, Spring 1995.

Reynolds, Michael. "Day of the Zealots." *Playboy*, Aug. 1995.

Richter, Paul. "Militia Fanatics No Patriots, Clinton Says." *San Francisco Chronicle*, May 6, 1995.

Ridgeway, James. "The Posse Goes to Washington." *Village Voice*, May 23, 1995.

Ridgeway, James, and Lenny Zeskind. "Revolution U.S.A.: The Far Right Militias Prepare for Battle." *Village Voice*, May 2, 1995.

Roddy, Dennis B. "Patriot Zealots Arm to Repel Unseen Foes." *Pittsburgh Post-Gazette*, Feb. 12, 1995.

Rosenthal, A. M. "Farrakhan Owned the Day." *New York Times*, Oct. 17, 1995.

Schneider, Rick. "Fearing a Conspiracy, Some Heed a Call to Arms." *New York Times*, Nov. 14, 1994.

———. "Manual for Terrorists Extols 'Greatest Cold-bloodedness.'" *New York Times*, Apr. 29, 1995.

"Terror in Oklahoma City: Official Responses; Statement by the President and Attorney General." *New York Times*, Apr. 20, 1995.

"This Land Is Whose Land?" *Newsweek*, Oct. 23, 1995.

Tolkin, Michael. "Something Wicked This Way Comes." *Village Voice*, Dec. 14, 1995.

Toner, Robin. "In Limbaughland, Election Jitters." *New York Times*, Nov. 3, 1994.

Verhovek, Sam Howe. "An Angry Bush Ends His Ties to Rifle Group." *New York Times*, May 11, 1995.

Wicker, Tom. "The Persistence of Inequality." *The New York Times Book Review*, Mar. 8, 1992.

Zeskind, Leonard. "Armed and Dangerous." *Rolling Stone*, Nov. 2, 1995.


REPORTS AND TESTIMONY

Anti-Defamation League. "Armed & Dangerous: Militias Take Aim at the Federal Government." New York, 1994.

Coalition for Human Dignity. "Patriot Games: Jack McLamb & Citizen Militias." Portland, Oregon, 1994.

Political Research Associates. "Armed Militias, Right Wing Populism & Scapegoating." Cambridge, Massachusetts, Apr. 1995.

Southern Poverty Law Center. "Klanwatch & Militia Task Force Intelligence Report." Vols. 1–80. Montgomery, Alabama, 1979–95.

Testimony of Morris S. Dees, Jr., before the United States Senate Committee on the Judiciary, Hearing on Terrorism in the United States: The Nature and Extent of the Threat and Possible Legislative Responses, Apr. 27, 1995.

Testimony of Brian J. Levin before the United States House Judiciary Committee, Crime Subcommittee, Hearing on

Anti-Government Terrorism in the United States: The Nature and Extent of the Threat and Possible Legislative Responses, Nov. 2, 1995.

U.S. Senate Subcommittee on Terrorism, Technology and Government Information, "Report on Ruby Ridge," Washington, D.C., 1995.


MISCELLANEOUS

The National Alliance. "What Is the National Alliance?" Hillsboro, West Virginia, 1993.

———. *National Alliance Bulletin.* Hillsboro, West Virginia, 1993–95.

———. *America's Dissident Voices.* Hillsboro, West Virginia, Apr. 1995

# Acknowledgments

I must first thank the people I grew up around, neighbors who gave me faith in my country. My rural community in Alabama faced hard times, but few hated the government or joined militias. They had faults, prejudices, and fears. In the end, though, they solved their problems with patience, hard work, and compromise. They were proud, patriotic Americans. They are my roots and inspiration.

I thank Richard Cohen, my friend and law partner, who is the unsung hero of *Gathering Storm*. He is an editor's editor. He guided me through some early false starts and made valuable contributions to the book.

I also want to thank Jim Corcoran for assisting with the book. I chose Jim to help because of his experience as a reporter in North Dakota during the Gordon Kahl incident. His award-winning book, *Bitter Harvest*, told a compelling story about the farm crisis of the early 1980s and the efforts of white supremacists to inject themselves into the issue. I also want to thank Jim's literary agent, Gail Ross, for making his involvement possible.

To my HarperCollins editors, Diane Reverand and Meaghan Dowling, and my literary agent, Carol Mann, I give thanks for their guidance and support.

There are so many more whose unselfish help made it possible for me to keep a full litigation schedule and write at the same time: Judy Bruno for printing the final manuscript; Linda Stringer for photo research; Danny Welch, Joe Roy, Mike Reynolds, Brian Levin, Cassandra Odum, Angie Lowry, Laurie Wood, Tawanda Shaw, Michelle Bramblett, Cindy Valieant, Sidney Hill, Lanita Crawford, Carey Parker, Lenny Zeskind, Bill Morlin, Jess Walter, and Chip Berlet for ideas and research; Rodney Diaz for graphic design; Joe Levin, Sara Bullard, and Eddie Ashworth for constructive editorial criticism; and Lynn Gomillion and Lillie Tucker for backing us all up.

Jim is most grateful to Nancy Brown Carroll who, by accepting the duty of chairing the Communications Department at Simmons College, gave him the time needed to work on this project; Jack and Carol Mullane, good neighbors whose fax machine helped maintain the link between Boston and Montgomery; and Donna Driesbach, whose computer expertise was called upon more than once and was willingly provided. Jim also extends a special thanks to his parents, Ken and Brenda, and friends Phil and Corinne Shute, Al Smith, Dan Connell, Kevin Carvell, Tamara Russell, Steve Singer, and Kim Borman, who were always close at hand when advice was sought or support was needed. And, most of all, Jim thanks Carolyn Shute for her deft editorial comments as well as her unwavering support, good humor, and love.

I could not have undertaken this project without the support of my wife, Elizabeth. Her kindness, love, and patience allowed me to put my whole heart into my work.

# Index